Editorial Freelancing

Rogers, Trumbull
Editorial freelancing:a practical guide/Trumbull Rogers

Copyright © 1995 by Trumbull Rogers

Library of Congress Catalog Card Number: 94-07451
ISBN: 0-9639260-1-2

Copyeditor: Henry W. Engel
Indexer: Henry W. Engel
Cover design: Guy J. Smith
Interior design and composition: Oh, Jackie!

Aletheia Publications, 38-15 Corporal Kennedy St., Bayside,
NY 11361

Printed in Canada

10 9 8 7 6 5 4 3

EDITORIAL FREELANCING
A Practical Guide

Trumbull Rogers

ALETHEIA
Publications

This book is dedicated to the thousands of editorial free-lancers who work tirelessly and usually anonymously to make the things we read a little more accurate, readable, and elegant.

"I have had to make a real effort to work semi-regular hours so that I do not end up working 7 days and 65–70 hours a week. I'm more productive and much happier. I think I got carried away with the 'flexibility' of freelancing for a number of years and forgot the pluses of having a routine, however loose."
—Karen Hammond, freelance editor and writer

". . . time is my most precious asset."
—Marcia Savin, freelance writer and proofreader

CONTENTS

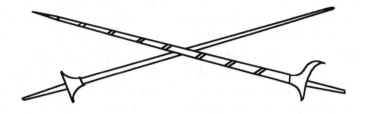

PREFACE

It was a drizzly evening late in July 1991. Two editorial freelancers, seated on imitation leather banquettes, faced each other across a table in the Malibu Diner. Almost directly across town, the clock on the MetLife tower had just struck 6:30; outside workers hurried homeward through the damp, gray dusk. Inside the restaurant, neighborhood people were rapidly filling the booths and the sound of chitchat clattered throughout the room, but the two freelancers, focused on their own conversation, were barely aware of their surroundings.

They were Laurie Lewis, chair of the Editorial Freelancers Association's Education Committee, and myself, and we were discussing a course I had agreed to lead on launching a freelance career. Strictly speaking, this book was also born on that night, because without the course I never would have thought of writing the book.

But why turn the course into a book in the first place? The answer to that question is twofold: (1) since *The Complete Guide to Editorial Freelancing,* by Carol L. O'Neill and Avima Ruder, went out of print there has been no book devoted solely to the concerns of editorial freelancers. (2) I thought it would be useful to make the information contained in the course available to as many editorial freelancers as possible.

Editorial Freelancing is designed for those who wish to start a career in editorial freelancing: that is, people who have lost their jobs in publishing but don't know how to get started as freelancers; people who have never liked the confinement of nine-to-five; parents at home who are raising small children or whose children have grown and are away at school or off on their own; and those who have lost their jobs due to early retirement, cutbacks, mergers, and other reorganizations.

The book begins with a brief discussion of editorial freelancing during the last twenty years, then moves on to such topics as editorial skills and specialties; setting up the office; basic equipment; electronic equipment; clients; the business aspects of freelancing; rates; billing; taxes; retirement plans; insurance; plus a few extras, including a brief look at current trends in publishing. There are also three appendixes containing a sample copyediting test, a sample style sheet, and lists of resources such as books and publications, organizations, courses, and grammar hotlines.

Editorial Freelancing is meant for use by both the novice and the experienced editorial worker. Thus, although the first three chapters are designed for people who are new to editorial work and to freelancing, the "old hands" might find some interesting tidbits in them.

This book makes no guarantees, however. The experiences and strategies described were gleaned by me and some of my colleagues during many years of freelancing. Also, the suggestions presented here are meant as guidelines, not as absolutes; success in freelancing, as in any other walk of life, comes through integrity, meeting deadlines, and hard work.

ACKNOWLEDGMENTS

Obviously, no one person has all of the knowledge and information necessary to write a book such as *Editorial Freelancing*. I am therefore grateful to the following individuals who were always available when I called, and who were generous with their help and encouragement.

First and foremost I want to thank Dorothy Kroll, without whose advice and support this book would have foundered early on, and Laurie Lewis, who persuaded me to teach the course out of which the book grew.

I am also indebted to Sheree Bykofsky, literary agent, and her reader Janet Rosen, both of whom helped me with the wording of the proposal; Enid Pearsons (Random House Reference Division), who read an early version of the proposal and suggested that I include definitions of the various editorial specialties and some material on computers; Jan Hall (Glencoe Publishing) for her enthusiastic support and much of the information for Appendix C3; my brother Danforth Rogers, attorney at law, for his generous and crucial advice on the wording of the contract; my niece Susan Luce Rogers, artist, for hand-lettering two of the figures; and Tamara Stiefel, who gave up one of her Saturday afternoons to run off an urgently needed copy of the proposal at a time when I was too busy to do it myself.

I am especially grateful to the following people for reviewing portions of the manuscript that deal with areas with which I'm not as familiar as they are: Allan Bateman (the musculature of the human body), John Berseth (health insurance), Sheila Buff (picture research), Jeannine Ciliotta (EFA history), my sister Grace Rogers (glucose replenishment in the brain), Patricia Godfrey (grammar books), Ellen Marsh (office organization), George Milite (business writing and editing), Bernice Petinatto (packagers and total-concept houses), Harriet Serenkin (computers), Frank Wieszner (life insurance), Barbara Zimmerman (rights and permissions), and the librarians at the Library of the American Institute of Certified Public Accountants.

I am also grateful to those who allowed me to use their names, words, and/or experiences: Denice Anderson, Carol Barko, David Hall, Karen Hammond, Al McCollough, Marian Rogers, Marilyn Salmansohn, Marcia Savin, David Schechter, Julie Stein, Richard Stiefel, and Sylvia Warren.

Others who offered support of various kinds were Jim and Marcia Beardsley, Steve Bohall, Bill Boland, Elaine Chubb, Sydney Wolfe Cohen, Justine Cullinan, Jack Dawson, Ellen Fuchs, Christine Hastings, Deborah Herbert, William Klein (CPA), Kevin Kollar (Citicorp Investment Services), Susan Lee (CPA), Roger Rogalin (Vice President, Association of American Publishers), Leslie Sharpe, Guy Smith, Martha Solonche, Hope Steele, Donn Teal, Jesse Weissman, and all my students, past and present.

Special thanks to my editor and publisher, Carolyn Smith, for her expert editing and for knowing exactly the right things to say to keep me on track during the writing process; Jerry Ralya for his perceptive review of the manuscript; and Henry Engel for his expert copyediting and excellent index. Finally, I want to thank my noneditorial friends and the members of my family for their love, encouragement, and understanding.

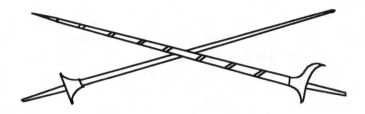

INTRODUCTION

As a profession freelancing has been around a lot longer than I've been practicing it, but when I started back in 1976, as far as I knew there was no central organized group where one could go for information and support, leaving freelancers feeling very isolated. In those days, when freelancers kept their rates and client lists secret for fear of being undercut and usurped, about the only way to learn about freelancing was by reading *The Complete Guide to Editorial Freelancing*, by Carol L. O'Neill and Avima Ruder.

Like so many others, however, my career began almost by accident. I had a regular job at the Institute of Electrical and Electronics Engineers (IEEE), where I had learned to copyedit, proofread both galleys and pages, do layout, and check repro.* I had left that job to finish work on a book I was coauthoring. Fortunately, the manuscript was finished and in the agent's hands in time for me to include a note to that effect on my Christmas cards.

Shortly after the new year began I received a call from the managing editor at the IEEE asking me if I'd like to do some freelance work for them. Eventually word got around the company, and the Standards Department also hired me for a couple of jobs. One day, while on my

---

* Reproduction proofs: Final, best quality proofs, which are used as camera copy.

way into the office to pick up some manuscripts, I thought, "What a great life. I wish I could be a freelancer." Then it hit me—I already was one! What I needed now was more clients—but how to get them? Even more important, how was I to approach book publishers? Past experience had taught me that publishing houses weren't interested unless you had a track record, and I was sure they would be put off by the fact that my only editing experience was in journals.

At about that time, Marian Rogers, to whom I was then married, introduced me to Mary Heathcote, a friend from her early days in publishing. Mary told us about an organization of freelancers she belonged to that held monthly meetings at St Luke's School in Greenwich Village. In fact, the speaker at their next meeting was to be Edwin Newman, who was going to speak on "Will America Be the Death of English?", the subtitle of his 1974 book *Strictly Speaking*. Wouldn't we like to come and perhaps meet Mr. Newman? Mary had been the (freelance) editor on his newest book, *A Civil Tongue*, and it was through her influence that he had agreed to speak, gratis, to the group.

This was my introduction to the Editorial Freelancers Association (EFA), although I didn't join until the following February. The speaker at that meeting was Marie Longyear, then Director of Editorial Services at the McGraw-Hill Book Company. A friend of Mary's introduced me to Marie, who told me to send her my résumé. In those days, McGraw trained their freelancers, so, after I passed the copyediting test, I had the good fortune of receiving solid grounding in textbook editing from Sylvia Warren, Marie's assistant and one of the best and most experienced editors in the business.

I go into such detail to recall the flavor of the times and to show one of the haphazard and unpremeditated ways in which some people become editorial freelancers. And the role of luck, because even with the best of intentions, freelancing is not a business in which one can easily survive without having or being able to quickly develop the skills that are necessary for success. Good freelancers are always in demand among in-house editors, and their identities are as closely guarded as were the names of clients in 1977. EFA and similar organizations throughout the country have gone a long way toward changing the latter attitude.

In the 1979 edition of *The Complete Guide to Editorial Freelancing*, O'Neill and Ruder wrote: "There is no organization where freelancers can meet to talk shop and exchange experiences, to share triumphs and gripes."[1] (Of course, EFA wrote them to correct this statement, and its name and address were duly added in the next printing.) Fortunately for me, what had seemed true in 1974, when the book was written, was no longer the case in 1977. As I've already stated, twenty years ago it was almost impossible to get colleagues to share vital information until you got to know them. Then they became more willing to reveal such basic information as what rate you should be charging, whom to talk to at various houses, and, on rare occasions, to suggest your name to a client when they were unable to take on a project.

But EFA wasn't operating in a vacuum. Other freelance organizations, some patterned on EFA, were springing up in other cities. One of these was the Manhattan Publishing Group (MPG), which EFA invited to be part of its May 1981 program on "The Freelance World"; the next year, however, MPG had vanished. Other freelance organizations included Media Circle (a forerunner of the Freelance Editorial Association) in Boston; Media Alliance in San Francisco; Freelance Editors' Association of Canada in Toronto; as well as Publication Services Guild in Atlanta. All these groups were founded for similar reasons: to provide a center for networking and social activities, plus support and services. Some of them, like MPG and Media Circle, went out of existence as a result of low enrollment or lack of commitment by their organizers. But sometimes, as in the case of Media Circle, new organizations rose, as it were, from their ashes, indicating a strong need for such support groups in the depersonalizing atmosphere caused by the continuing conglomeration of the publishing industry from the mid-1970s to the present day. In other words, freelancers, like other groups, needed professional associations where they could air their grievances, share their experiences, and discover new coping strategies.

Those groups that succeeded best were the ones that didn't strike an adversary pose but quietly worked with in-house editors and such groups as the Association of American Publishers (AAP) to improve the lot of freelancers while gaining respect and influence in the industry. Editors and other industry representatives were invited to participate on panels where freelancers could speak directly to them and give them résumés; at the same time, the panelists could speak directly to freelancers about what they expected of them as well as the things freelancers sometimes do that cost them continuing employment—for example, acting like the type of editor referred to by Hugh Leonard, the Irish playwright, when he said, "Life's headiest drive is not love's orgasm, or hate's dagger, but one person's need to change another person's copy."

Why am I talking about these organizations at such length? Quite simply because I want to show how editorial freelancing has grown and developed over the last twenty years, especially in cities where groups like EFA have come into being. These organizations have had a tremendous influence on the course of freelancing as a profession, transforming it from one of almost total isolation to one where isolation is tempered by free and open information exchange.

Freelancing will continue to evolve as increasing numbers of magazines and publishing houses become more involved with computer technology and interactive projects. In the almost fifteen years since EFA's first meeting on the use of computers and their future in publishing, held in November 1980,* people have been predicting the disappearance of both hard-copy editing and books as we know them. (In fact, this has been predicted about books since at least the 1960s.) Everything, they say, will be available on screen. If this were to occur, it would be a tragedy comparable to few other extinctions. Not only would it reduce the quality of life, but who could let their imagination run while reading from a computer screen? There is a chapter in John Steinbeck's unfinished rendering of the Arthurian legend that filled my living room with deep forests and the sounds of clanking armor as heavily weighted horses shuffled along paths ankle-deep in last fall's leaves. Sunlight filtered through the treetops where birds played among the branches, and somewhere nearby there was the gushing sound of a stream in full spate. At the time I was seated in a comfortable chair in my living room, the book illuminated by a single lamp, the rest of the room in deep shadow. Can you imagine getting the same effect while reading from a computer screen? But the reality is that in perhaps five years (the pundits are now saying) hard-copy editing will be an artifact of another vanished golden time.

But what about books themselves? Will they, too, disappear into the electronic maw? Current thinking says "no," because, as Peter Givler, Director of Ohio State University Press, has pointed out: "The most durable of electronic media, at best guess, will last 20 to 25 years; already many archives are readable only on equipment that is no longer manufactured."[2] Many books, on the other hand, have lasted hundreds of years and are still readable.

All of which brings me at last to the point of this book: during my early years as a freelancer I learned the tricks and "secrets" of my trade in a kind of catch-as-catch-can way. This is one reason I agreed to conduct the course on launching a freelance business when the chair of EFA's Education Committee first broached the possibility to me. Ever

---

* The year before, at the May meeting, Herbert Mitgang, who wrote the book column for the *New York Times*, told EFA that "even though learning to cope with his Teleram (computer terminal) has been nearly enough to drive [him] back to the quill pen, he feels that the new technology will, in the long run, mean more books and more work for more people." Marian Rogers, "Good Company," *EFA Newsletter*, May 1979.

since my early days in EFA, when I listened in bewilderment while members resisted sharing information, it seemed obvious to me that the cause of freelancing could only be helped by making as much information available to as many freelancers as possible. Ignorance is not bliss; it is self-limiting, as too many freelancers have found out the hard way.

I think it was on the way home from the inaugural session of my course on setting up a freelance business that the idea of turning the course into a book first occurred to me. It has taken a long time to convert that idea into a reality. Although this book is based mostly on my personal experiences and those of some of my colleagues, I have tried to make it as accurate and up-to-date as possible. I hope you find the result both enjoyable and useful.

NOTES

1. *The Complete Guide to Editorial Freelancing,* Carol L. O'Neill and Avima Ruder, Barnes & Noble Books, New York, 1979, p. 7.
2. John F. Baker, "UPs View Issues of Survival in Electronic Age," *Publishers Weekly,* July 11, 1994, p. 17.

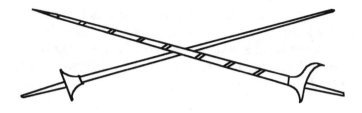

THE EDITORIAL SMORGASBORD

1

Welcome to the wonderful world of editorial freelancing! As the name implies, the first freelancer* was a kind of soldier of fortune—a knight who was unattached to any lord, and whose business card read: "Have lance, will travel." In other words, he was for hire by anyone who could pay his rate. In modern terms, "freelancer" is another way of saying "consultant."

After knights went out of fashion, it was an easy step in the evolution of language to apply the term to anyone who has special knowledge or abilities that he or she offers for sale to the world at large. For example, as we'll see later in this book, editorial freelancers do not restrict their activities to established firms, but on occasion also work for individuals—graduate students seeking help with a thesis, writers who want a manuscript edited before submission, or individuals who need help designing and writing a brochure. The possibilities are virtually limitless.

Since this chapter is designed for those who are new to editorial work or to freelancing, readers with more experience may want to skip ahead. For the rest, let's begin by taking a look at the various specialties involved in the editorial process—the editorial smorgasbord, as it were.

---

*The term "free lance" was first used in this context by Sir Walter Scott in his novel *Ivanhoe;* in feudal times the term used was "free companions."[1]

Before starting, however, it might be instructive to note the meanings of some common editorial terms such as *caret* and *stet* (both derived from Latin), which mean, respectively, "there is lacking" and "let it stay," while the Latin word *dele* means "delete it." Another interesting, though little known term is *wayzgoose* (word origin unknown), which is a printers' annual outing or entertainment.* The term is still in use in the printing trade today.

EDITORIAL TYPES AND TERMS

What is an editor? Freelancer David Hall recently reminded me of one definition: "An editor is merely a device to turn coffee into books." But this tells only part of the story— especially since, strictly speaking, editorial freelancers drink everything from water ("I tell myself it is a hot fudge sundae," says one aquarian) to diet soda to herb tea while they're working. Although to many people the duties of a copyeditor seem to parallel those of an English teacher, Laura Horowitz has often told her copyediting students at George Washington University: "Knowledge of editorial style is what distinguishes the copyeditor from the English teacher."[2]

You will find both the terms *editor* and *copyeditor* in the previous paragraph. This begins to show the diversity of editorial functions. While these two terms are often used interchangeably, to anyone working in publishing they have distinct connotations, though perhaps not as distinct as they once were. When I started freelancing in the mid-1970s, one still heard it said that copyeditors earned less than those who did editing who earned less than those who did heavy editing who earned less than those who did rewriting. In fact, in those days you still heard that manuscripts† were edited before they were copyedited, the copyeditor being the last person in the editorial chain to see the manuscript before it went to the compositor.‡

Perhaps it will be easier to deal with the myriad editorial specialties if we first list them in the approximate sequence in which they would be performed in the bookmaking process.

---

* From *Webster's Third New International Dictionary*, G. & C. Merriam Company, Springfield, Mass., 1976.

† According to Oliver Herford (1863–1935), an English-born American writer and illustrator, a manuscript is "something submitted in haste and returned at leisure."

‡ Sometimes the word "printer" is used when "compositor" is meant. Today, many compositors, who do composition and who are involved in the early stages of production, also do printing, but the distinction between the functions remains.

1. Research
2. Developmental editing
3. Writing of whatever type (i.e., book, article, speech, ghost)
4. Manuscript evaluation
5. Translation
6. Picture research
7. Design
8. Production editing
9. Rewriting
10. Flap/jacket/promotional copy writing
11. Line editing
12. Copyediting
13. Rights and permissions
14. Layout (dummying*)
15. Galley proofreading
16. Page proofreading
17. Indexing
18. Abstracting and abridging

Because this book focuses on editorial freelancing, however, we will discuss them in a slightly different order.

Traditional Editing

In 1977 the Association of American University Presses compiled and published a book called *One Book/Five Ways, The Publishing Procedures of Five University Presses*.† Two of the most striking features of this book were that although the five companies were given the same manuscript, no two sample copyedited pages were the same, and that each company came up with a different design for the example book. While on reflection the latter may not be too surprising, one would expect the editing to be uniform in all five instances. The fact that it was not shows that, although the parameters of editing are universal, their execution differs with each individual applying them. In other words, every editor approaches and handles a manuscript—even the same manuscript—in a unique way. Sometimes these differences might be

---

* A dummy is created by cutting up a set of galley proofs and laying them out on dummy paper in exactly the way that the final printed version should appear; that is, with the precise spacing and with figures and tables in place.

† See Appendix C1 and Chapter 3 for complete citations of the job-related books referred to in this chapter.

determined by the instructions the copyeditor receives from the client, but even when these instructions are the same, differences persist. Therefore one might conclude that there is no one right way of copy-editing a manuscript, although there is most assuredly a wrong way!

Since editorial freelancers deal mostly with project editors, let's begin with a brief description of their duties.

Project Editor (sometimes called editorial supervisor, production editor, or production manager). This editor is an endangered species at many publishing houses, as companies continue to downsize and rely increasingly on freelancers. The project editor's job is to oversee production for a project. He or she is in contact with the author over styling decisions, troublesome questions of expression, missing chapters or artwork; serves as liaison with the compositor; hires and supervises the freelance copyeditor, proofreader, and indexer; works with the art and production departments and the designer; and keeps track of the flow of work to and from all the parties involved, including the author. Often overworked, the project editor usually has to deal with several books at a time. Sometimes freelancers are hired to do this work, but usually for only one project at a time.

Now let's consider the areas of editing with which most freelancers are involved: developmental editing, line editing, and copyediting.

Developmental editing. As indicated in the list in the last section, developmental editing is done early in the publication process. Although many development editors are on staff, many also work freelance. As their title implies, they develop projects, usually college textbooks. The development editor is responsible for many phases of book management, from manuscript evaluation to editing of the final manuscript. Besides serving as liaison between the author and the publisher, the development editor also analyzes competing books, edits the completed chapters, and evaluates the reviews.* Sometimes a development editor writes portions of the text, including sidebars or "boxes," chapter summaries, and figure or photo captions.

Line editing. Line editing is defined differently depending on whom you talk to—it is also called heavy editing, substantive editing, developmental editing, and just plain editing. Line editors evaluate manuscripts and make suggestions for improvement; thus they are hidden partners of the author. In the words of Nancy Evans, "Most editors agree that it takes two to edit: an editor who believes that a good book can be made

---

* These are not book reviews in the usual sense, but evaluations written by experts in the field who have been given copies of the manuscript and asked to comment on matters such as the appropriateness of the coverage and reading level.

better and a writer who is serious about his or her prose."[3] To summarize, the line editor is responsible for ensuring that the work is generally accurate, covers the subject completely, and is written in a suitable tone.

Editing. *Editing* and *editor* are catch-all words that are often used as shortened forms of the terms *line editing* and *copyediting.* *Editor* is also sometimes synonymous with *manager,* as in the editor of a small-town newspaper, or *coordinator,* as in the editor of an anthology. Editing, and copyediting, also come in various gradations: light, medium, and heavy—anything beyond heavy editing is rewriting, which was formerly a separate function but is now often performed by a copyeditor.

The three gradations of editing can be defined as follows:

Light editing. In a light edit, the editor (or copyeditor) makes sure that the manuscript is correct and consistent. In other words, the editor does the minimum amount of work necessary to ensure that a manuscript is grammatically and factually correct; is correctly marked and coded for the compositor; and is free of jargon, sexism, slander, obscenity, and prejudice. The editor also makes sure that art and text correspond and that text citations (called callouts) for figures, tables, footnotes, and cross-references are noted in the margin; that references, bibliographies, and footnotes are correctly numbered; and that all necessary information for them has been supplied.

Medium editing. Here the editor (or copyeditor) makes sure that the writing is clear and concise. A more thorough edit is done in order to reduce wordiness and get rid of triteness, obscurities and confusing language, vague generalizations, tense changes, and mixed metaphors; make sure that elements in a series are parallel; improve organization, word choices, fluency (without rewriting), and transitions; and make sure that headings are parallel in construction, number, and frequency within each chapter.

Heavy editing. Here the breadth and depth of the editing is again expanded to make sure that the manuscript is accurate and covers the material appropriately. The editor (or copyeditor) must make sure that each chapter is organized coherently and logically; get rid of gaps, redundancies, jargon, and other inappropriate material; query the author about uneven coverage; make sure the tone, focus, and use of background material are appropriate and consistent; make sure terms, definitions, and headings are introduced as appropriate, and, if necessary, properly integrate figures and tables. In addition, he or she might sometimes be asked to spot-check the accuracy of basic facts or make recommendations for new and/or different art and subject matter.

Copyediting. Originally, copyediting consisted of doing basic fact checking; correcting grammar and usage; marking trademarks correctly;* checking callouts to be sure they correspond correctly with the cited table, figure, footnote, or reference and that all this material has been received; checking for basic consistency; final key- and typemarking† of the manuscript; and keeping a complete style sheet (see Appendix B for a sample). Figure 1 shows a sample copyedited page.

Most publishers, however, expect copyeditors to perform some additional tasks such as suggesting art to be added or deleted, creating a list of typesetting codes, and reorganizing and/or rewriting portions of the text. In the interests of streamlining the editorial process to meet shorter scheduling deadlines and to reduce expenditures, publishing companies have gradually merged some editing functions with those of the copyeditor. In effect, the copyeditor, who was once expected to perform very specific tasks, has become a jack-of-all-trades, performing a large catalog of tasks from basic fact-checking to heavy editing/rewriting.

According to William Bridgwater, a past editor in chief of Columbia University Press, the copyeditor must have the following five qualities: (1) a love of books, that is, "the touch and feel of books"; (2) respect for authors—"The worst disease that can attack a copy editor is arrogance toward authors"; (3) an eye for detail; (4) a thorough familiarity with both the English language and current usage, yet not overly rigid in their application; and (5) curiosity, an attribute that helps the copyeditor grow in professionalism.[4]

Even though copyeditors are charged with making sure facts and word choices are correct, the author still makes the final decisions. For example, if the author has given birth and/or death dates that differ from those in standard sources, the copyeditor needs to query the author as to which source he or she wants to follow. Word choices, however, can be a fine line. If an author's first language is not English, he or she often needs help in this area. My high school English teacher told of an incident that occurred when he was teaching English to newly arrived immigrants. He asked the students to write a theme about an incident they had witnessed since arriving in the United States. One man, in describing a fire in a neighboring building, wrote the following: "The fireman then ran into the burning building and

---

* This is very important, because when a brand name becomes generic through popular use, the company loses the trademark protection. *Rollerblade* is a current example of a trademark in jeopardy—the word *Rollerblade* is a trademark; the proper generic term is *in-line skates* or *in-line skating*. You can verify the status of a term by checking it in the *Trade Names Dictionary* or calling the U.S. Trademark Association and asking for trademark information.

† *Keymarking* is another word for coding, wherein the copyeditor marks a code such as an A (for a first-level head) beside the appropriate element; *typemarking* refers to writing the actual specification beside each element.

(A) RESULTS

(B) 1 Sensory functions

(C) a) *Mononuclear tests*

Visual acuity with best correction for distance and near [close up] was significantly lower in dyslexics than in normal readers. Of the normal readers 94 % [percent] had a distance acuity of 1.0 (20/20) or better, but only 83 % [percent] of the dyslexics. For near acuity the corresponding numbers were 99% [percent] and 87% [percent], respectively. Further details are shown in Table 1 ["one"].

Contrast sensitivity was lower in the dyslexic group than in controls, in the low (1.5–3 cycles per degree) as well as in the high spatial frequency range (18 cycles per degree), but not for medium spatial frequencies. These differences were statistically significant (Wilcoxon–Mann–Whitney test).

(C) b) Binocular tests

Stereopsis was normal (60″ [double prime] or better) in 57 dyslexics and 56 normal readers. Defects of stereoscopic vision were [was] seen mainly in children with strabismus.

Ocular dominance and its stability. We found no difference in the stability of ocular dominance between dyslexics and normal readers (Table 2), if stability was defined as dominance of one eye at least 8 times out of 10 tests[16]. A strong left dominance, with all 10 trials favouring this eye, was much more common than a strong right dominance in both groups of children (Table 2). A statistical analysis (Fisher's exact test) showed no significant difference between stable and unstable ocular dominance in either group.

Figure 1. Example of a copyedited manuscript page. (This page is reproduced with the kind permission of The New York Academy of Sciences.)

came out pregnant." What he had meant to say was that the fireman came out "with child" or "carrying a child."

But suppose the author is a native English speaker and the sentence reads: "A light breeze wafted through Emily's hair." A copyeditor might be tempted to change "wafted" to "played" or "ruffled," but should resist the impulse. Arbitrary changes of this nature often raise the ire of authors—"What makes this pipsqueak think his choice is better than mine? I'm the author here!" The copyeditor can, however, either make the change and ask the author if it is okay, or just query the author as to whether such a change might be desirable. A diplomatically worded suggestion is apt to do the trick without raising the author's hackles. The best query suggests that the change is what the author meant to write in the first place. In other words, the copy-editor should not appear to impose his or her will on the author or to rewrite the author's prose to suit the copyeditor's "inner ear." Queries can either be written on the page (if it's short, such as "AU: Change OK?") or on an editorial "flag" (usually in the form of a Post-it).

Although the level of editing determines the speed at which a copyeditor is expected to work, a good average rate is eight pages an hour. Even so, different companies have different requirements about the number of pages they want completed (turned) per hour. One editor noted that when technical material is involved, her company would consider the editor to be working too fast if he or she turned more than three pages an hour; another company requires its freelancers to turn no fewer than ten pages an hour, no matter the nature of the material. Most in-house editors are skilled at judging how many pages a freelancer should be able to complete in an hour, given the type of material and the level of editing involved. Once when working in-house I received a completed manuscript from a freelance copyeditor along with an invoice that gave a lower number of pages turned per hour than was reasonable considering the level of editing requested and the amount of work done. Since this amounted to padding the bill, we paid the invoice, but did not hire the freelancer again.

Occasionally a copyeditor will be asked to typemark as well as code the manuscript. Coding should be sufficient instruction to the compositor, as each code [e.g., NL (or LN) for numbered list] is fully described in the design specifications.

A final tip regarding copyediting projects: Often when you've finished a project the client will send a messenger to pick it up. In such instances you should write "BY MESSENGER" on the outside of the package, under the client's address. If, however, you are returning the project yourself, you should write "BY HAND" instead.

Proofreading

Although etymologically speaking the term *editor* originated in the 1640s, the earliest known reference to proofreading is a contract signed by an author in 1499 that makes him responsible for correcting the proofs of his book. From the outside, proofreading looks so simple that virtually everyone thinks they can do it as a sideline to earn extra income. But it takes not only the skills of a copyeditor, especially a thorough knowledge of the English language, grammar, and usage, but also a sense of how books and/or magazines are made to be a good and successful proofreader.

Even though the term *proofreading* preceded *editing* by 150 years, today one often gets the impression that it is considered less important than editing, an impression reflected in the fact that proofreaders are paid less than copyeditors and are invariably blamed for errors made by the compositor *after* all the proofs have been read.

Also contributing to this frustrating condition is the fact that proofreading can be done according to four different styles, each less effective than the preceding one: two-person proofreading; proofreading by one person against copy; cold reading; and spot-checking. The type used in any given instance is usually dictated by a combination of financial and scheduling considerations.

Two-person proofreading. In this style, two people sit facing each other, one with the edited manuscript and the other with the galleys.* The person with the galleys reads aloud everything that appears on the page, including punctuation and any styling elements, such as heads. The other person reads the manuscript silently, interrupting whenever there is a discrepancy between the two, such as a copyediting change overlooked by the keyboarder. After a few galleys, the two change positions so that they don't get stale or careless. This style is considered to be the most effective way of proofreading, but it has a number of disadvantages: (1) it requires the use of two workers; (2) it makes most sense if it's done in-house, often by staff members who also may be inexperienced at proofreading, such as secretaries or entry-level editorial personnel; (3) if a company wants to use a freelancer, it has to hire two if the work is to be done out-of-house.

Proofreading against copy. In this method the proofreader places the galleys and edited manuscript side-by-side on the desk and reads one against the other, word for word. This method, while highly effective, has the disadvantage of being time-consuming. The proofreader also has to take frequent breaks in order to keep his or her eyes fresh.

---

* So called because the flat oblong tray the type was originally placed in resembled a kind of ship called a galley.

Cold read. This method is perhaps the most widely used today, because an alert proofreader can pick up the majority of the errors and it is faster than reading against copy. Here the proofreader again places the galleys and edited manuscript side-by-side on the desk, but this time he or she reads only the galleys. When something questionable is encountered, the proofreader checks the printed version. The disadvantage of this method is that a sentence or part of a sentence that has been omitted or accidentally deleted may be missed if the copy being read makes sense. For example, suppose the manuscript said: "The boy entered the room and stopped short. He was amazed at how fresh and beautiful everything looked. The boy entered the wardrobe and immediately encountered the back wall. No secret passage here!" but what the keyboarder copied was this: "The boy entered the wardrobe and immediately encountered the back wall. No secret passage here!" This kind of error is very common when two proximal sentences begin the same way.

Spot-checking. This is a "quick-and-dirty" proofreading style in which the proofreader checks certain elements, such as titles, heads, figure captions, tables, displayed math, footnotes, and references, and scans the text, only occasionally "tuning in" to what is on the page. You'd be amazed at the number of errors that will pop out at an experienced proofreader using this method—but many more may be missed.

The final two stages of proofreading, which are usually done in-house, are checking repro and blues. Although everyone involved wants to produce the best and most accurate product possible, the only corrections that will be allowed at these stages are those involving spelling errors, errors in fact or substance, and some errors in consistency, such as a name change or a change in math (e.g., x^2 to x^{-2}). Other changes are not made, mainly because it is so expensive to make them, but also because editors don't want to take the time and risk failing to meet the bound-book date.

Proofreaders sometimes forget that they are not copyeditors. While they should be alert to the same kinds of errors that copyeditors are responsible for correcting, they shouldn't fix these errors arbitrarily, but should bring them to the attention of the in-house editor. An example of a change that will probably have to be made is changing "florescence" to "fluorescence," depending on the context; changes that probably won't be made involve the serial comma and the use of "data" as singular, especially if these usages are consistent throughout. Proofreaders must navigate a fine line here, and the temptation will always be toward changing the copy. Most often, however, they will have to restrain their impulses and follow style decisions made at an earlier stage. Therefore a general rule might be to correct all typos and other typesetting errors, as well as errors in grammar and syntax, and query everything else you feel is wrong, either directly to the in-house editor or on an editorial flag.

Under normal circumstances, a proofreader should be able to turn 5 to 7 long galleys per hour, or 125 to 175 per week, working 5 hours a day for a 5-day week. If you're working with page-size galleys, 8 galleys an hour might be a good average, or, again working 5 hours a day for a 5-day week, 200 galleys a week. A freelance proofreader who reads mostly page proofs told me that he turns about 100 pages a day for a total of 400 to 500 pages a week, which is probably about average.

In spite of everything I've just said, proofreading can often be an easy way to segue into a career as an editorial freelancer. This is because proofreading jobs are fairly abundant—check the want ads in your local paper—and occur in a wide range of professions. Employers are therefore more apt to take a chance on an inexperienced applicant if he or she demonstates basic abilities on a proofreading test and otherwise creates a good impression. Once you're working as a proofreader, you will be developing many of the skills necessary for copyediting, and so will eventually be able to take this next step up the editorial ladder.

In concluding this section, I want to introduce you to a common occurrence in proofreading that I call Gordon's Rule, after the editor who first pointed it out to me.

Gordon's Rule: When two typos occur close together, the proofreader will see and correct the first one but miss the second.

The reasons for this are twofold: (1) the proofreader will be so caught up in dealing with the first error that upon returning to reading the galley his or her attention won't be fully focused on the text, and (2) having just found one error, the proofreader won't be expecting to encounter another one so soon.

Other Options

There are two points about editorial freelancing that are worth emphasizing: (1) freelancing is a business, and (2) the more you know about the publishing process, the more valuable you will be to your clients. A corollary to the latter point is that the more editorial skills you possess, the more apt you are to be continually employed, not to mention interested. In some areas publishing is cyclical. Textbooks are a prime example, since they all need to be ready for adoption at approximately the same time(s) of year. In order to meet these deadlines, therefore, textbooks are generally all copyedited at one time and proofread at another. Thus it's easy to see that if you work in this field as a copyeditor you'll be kept frantically busy for several weeks, and then your clients will stop calling while their projects enter the next phase of the cycle. If, however, you also proofread, you'd be busy during the proofreading phase as well. And if you did indexing, you could be involved in yet another phase. But even though you wanted to specialize in textbooks, the work might not be sufficient to carry you through the entire year. Therefore, you'd either want to find clients in other areas, say, professional and/or reference books, or expand your range of editorial skills. This section will give you an idea of what some of these other skills are.

Writing . . .

There are so many good books about writing—business, technical, freelance, script, mystery, children's—and its various aspects that I'm only going to suggest some of the areas you might consider. Perhaps one of the best books for aspiring writers is *Becoming a Writer*, by Dorothea Brande.

Since everything we read has to be written by someone, there is a virtually limitless pool of possibilities for writers, some of which are:

1. *Business:* annual reports, business forecasts, brochures, and the like.
2. *Copywriting,* including, but not limited to, advertising, promotional, and book-cover flap and jacket copy.
3. *Documentation,* especially for computer hardware and software, but also for TVs, CDs, and any other appliance that requires assembly and/or operating instructions.
4. *Ghostwriting:* writing something for someone else for publication under that person's name. Can be as extensive as an "autobiography" or as limited as an after-dinner speech. The main point here is that the work is done for a fee, usually a project rate and/or a share in the royalties, but otherwise your name will not be associated with the finished work.
5. *Grant proposal writing:* researching and targeting funding sources, deciphering the request for proposal, and organizing and writing the grant. This can be for a wide variety of clients, such as corporations,

small businesses, start-up business ideas, education-
al and medical institutions, and artists and writers,
to name some of the most obvious ones. For more
detailed information, see *Grants for Nonprofit
Organizations,* by Eleanor Gilpatrick, *Grants for the
Arts,* by Virginia P. White, and *Grants and Awards
Available to American Writers 1992/1993* (17th ed.).

6. *Newsletters:* researching and writing articles in
   focused areas, such as pharmaceuticals. In some cases
   you might write and create the entire newsletter.
7. *Newspapers,* such as shoppers' guides and neighborhood newspapers, including the ones circulated for
   free—even New York's *Street News,* which is sold by
   the homeless in the subways, railroad stations, bus
   terminals, and on street corners, has to be written by
   someone.
8. *Scriptwriting,* not only screen and theatrical, but for
   promotional videos, corporate shows, and the like.
9. *Speechwriting:* researching and writing speeches for
   politicians, corporate executives, and others.

I'm sure a glance around your apartment will suggest other writing
possibilities. Some ways of finding these jobs are described later in this
book; any good book on freelance writing will suggest others not covered here.

... And the Rest of the Feast

The same caveat holds for editorial work as for writing: everything
that is written has to be edited and proofread by someone. Sometimes
researched, translated, indexed, and possibly more. While some of
these jobs may not be available to freelancers, many more are; the trick
is to determine which ones are lucrative enough to warrant your attention. Some ways of seeking them out are suggested later in this book
(see, e.g., Chapters 5 and 6).

In the meantime, following are definitions of the editorial specialties.

Abstracting and abridging are basically the processes of condensing an
article, book, or other written matter to summarize its main points.
Especially in scholarly and professional journal articles, abstracts are
often collected and published separately as guides to the literature. An
abstract should therefore be short, in a neutral voice, and able to stand
on its own. Thus, it should not contain figure or reference citations (see

Figure 2 for examples of correct and incorrect abstract formats). Examples of abridgments are the Reader's Digest Condensed Books series and the classic literature that has been condensed for high school consumption, such as Sir Walter Scott's *Ivanhoe*, Herman Melville's *Moby Dick*, and Victor Hugo's *Les Misérables*.

Design is creating an effective method of rendering books, articles, or other printed matter graphically. This usually takes the form of choosing type specifications, which specify the typesizes, typefaces, and weights for the various elements of a book, plus the spaces around them. These specs also include the codes for keymarking.

Copyeditors and proofreaders should be able to read these specifications, although examples of typeset pages (called sample pages) are usually included with the manuscript so that the copyeditor and proofreader will be able to see how the various elements will look and be spaced when set in print.

The design begins when someone, most often the project editor, goes through the manuscript and flags examples of all the recurring elements—heads; tables; footnotes, references, and captions; displayed mathematics, such as equations, theorems, corollaries; examples; problems/exercises sections; and so forth—that need designing. This is called a design survey. The actual design can as easily be done by a freelance designer as by an in-house designer (who might also do the survey) in the Art or Production Department. For example, when a book is being handled by a packager,* the design would probably be done by a freelancer.

Desktop publishing is the process of using a computer to combine text and graphics to produce a final product. The process can include some or all of the following steps, depending on the project: writing the copy, typesetting the copy, creating and/or reproducing the art, and doing the design and layout. As a desktop publisher you would be using specialized hardware and software to produce all manner of publications, including but not limited to newsletters, books, magazines/journals, audiovisual products, and promotional and advertising copy.

Indexing is the process of creating a system for locating information in printed material, such as an alphabetical listing of subjects or names, as well as other categories. The index can be in one of two basic forms: a com-

---

* Packagers do everything from generating the idea to producing the finished product. They often need writers, copyeditors, proofreaders, picture researchers, designers, and occasionally factual researchers. On the other hand, although they sometimes function the same as packagers, total-concept houses generally take manuscripts from a publisher, hire freelance copyeditors and proofreaders to work on them, and produce camera-ready copy, which is then sent back to the publisher for printing and binding.

(a) Incorrect

Abstract.   In our article we portray the life of
Arthur Rimbaud (born Jean-Nicolas-Arthur; 1854-
1891) as one of ectasy and debauchery, mostly
self-willed and self-induced. We show that he
willingly allowed himself to be seduced by the
older poet, Paul Verlaine (1844-1896), another of
France's lost souls, to further these ends. We
use extensive quotes from Enid Starkie's classic
biography of Rimbaud,[1] as well as from Rimbaud's
poems and letters as translated by Paul Schmidt,[2]
and especially *Une Saison en enfer*. We also use
the recently released transcript of the notorious
trial following Verlaine's shooting and wounding
of Rimbaud in Brussels. We do not, however, cover
the later years of Rimbaud's life, spent as a
vagabond, coffee merchant, explorer, and gunrun-
ner for King Menelek of Abyssinia.

(b) Correct

Abstract: The life of Arthur Rimbaud is
portrayed as one of ectasy and debauchery, mostly
self-willed and self-induced. It is shown that he
willingly allowed himself to be seduced by the
older poet, Paul Verlaine, to further these ends.
Both Enid Starkie's classic biography of Rimbaud
and Rimbaud's poems, especially *Une Saison en
enfer*, and letters are extensively quoted. The
authors also refer to the recently released transcript of the trial following Verlaine's shooting
and wounding of Rimbaud in Brussels. The later
years of Rimbaud's life are not covered.

Figure 2. Examples of an abstract. (a) Incorrect form; (b) correct form.

puterized database or a written document. There are two basic styles of index, indented and run in, and two basic ways of alphabetizing them, by letter and by word (see Figure 3). Indexes used to be made by first writing down entries on 3 x 5-inch index cards, then organizing the cards alphabetically, and then editing and typing them up in the desired format so that it achieved the necessary number of lines. Today there are several computer programs for indexing that help in most of the scut work, such as alphabetizing, thus making indexes easier and less time-consuming to create.

In book publishing, the index is the author's responsibility; that is to say, authors either create it themselves, find someone to create it, or let the publisher hire a freelancer, in which case the cost is charged back to the author's royalties. A good index is more difficult to compile than it may seem, and since a good index can measurably contribute to a book's usability and sales, publishers tend to discourage authors from doing their own indexes, though they must offer them the opportunity to do so. There are other reasons for not wanting authors to do their own indexes. The author may not produce a usable document, or may bog down part way through; both situations would necessitate starting over with a freelance indexer. In either event precious time is lost, thereby costing the book adoptions, if it's a textbook, or reserved shelf space in bookstores.

Indexers charge either by the hour, by the page, or by the line. For more information on indexing, see, for example, Chapter 17 of *The Chicago Manual of Style* (14th ed.) or Part II of *Words into Type* (3rd ed.).

Layout is the process of producing a dummy or a picture of the publication or cover in question. If it's a dummy, it will be laid out according to the design specifications created by a designer. Page layout can also be done on a computer, as in desktop publishing. On the other hand, for a cover or other graphic, such as a logo, a sketch will often suffice.

Manuscript evaluation is the analysis of a manuscript prior to publication to seek out its strengths, weaknesses, and trouble spots. A classic example of manuscript evaluation is contained in a single sentence by Dr. Samuel Johnson: "Your manuscript is both good and original, but the part that is good is not original and the part that is original is not good." Although succinct, this report would not suffice today, because the purpose of manuscript evaluation is not necessarily to determine the publishability of a manuscript, but rather whether it's publishable in its present form. Perhaps the book needs to be extensively reorganized and/or rewritten; perhaps it would benefit by an expanded art program; perhaps the author's English or writing style needs help; perhaps certain portions of the text would be more accessible if they were converted to tables; perhaps the author uses a number of tables that are

(a) The letter-by-letter form	(b) The word-by-word form
roscoe	roscoe
Rose, Billy	Rose, Billy
Rose, Pete	rose chafer
rosebay	rose cut
rose-breasted	rose fever
grosbeak	Rose, Pete
rose chafer	rosebay
rose cut	rose-breasted
rose fever	grosbeak
rosemary	rosemary
rough fist	rough fist
roughhouse	rough leg
rough leg	roughhouse
royal blue	royal blue
royalism	royal jelly
royal jelly	royalism
royalty	royalty
RPV (remotely	RPV (remotely
piloted vehicle)	piloted vehicle)
rrhea	rrhea
rRNA (ribosomal	rRNA (ribosomal
ribonucleic acid)	ribonucleic acid)
rubber-stamp	rubber stamp
rubber stamp	rubber-stamp
rubbing	rubbing

Figure 3. Examples of two ways of alphabetizing an index. (a) By letter; (b) by word.

really lists, or figures that are really displayed text. As an evaluator, your final report should include all of the points mentioned here, plus anything else you consider noteworthy, such as missing permissions and art work.

Picture research is the process of creating the photo program for a printed work. By this I mean planning, choosing, and arranging for the use of appropriate photographs and illustrations, and then supplying these materials to the client. In the process you may have to do some related research as well as write the captions, but you would not be responsible for doing any of the photography or creating any of the other art. Three major factors in picture research are your time, your client's budget, and the quality of the pictures.[5] The two most fertile areas to look for freelance work are trade and textbooks.

There are several established sources for pictures, such as museums, commercial stock companies, and public, government, and industrial libraries.[5] These pictures are not available for free, nor, in the case of libraries, does the archive always hold the copyrights. Thus it is necessary to incur fees—reproduction and print fees; research fees and service charges; holding fees; fees for loss or damage[6]—and to carry out thorough searches for copyright owners and to secure written permission to use their pictures, cartoons, or illustrations. Because they're asking you to clear permissions on photos, etc., your clients may also ask you to clear some for other illustrative material at the same time. On the matter of fees, it is very important that you indemnify yourself against loss or damage of the pictures.[5] There are also hidden costs for mailing, picture preservation, telephone calls, and, sometimes, office space and clerical staff.[5] It is therefore very important that you keep complete, accurate, and detailed records.

Picture researchers can charge by the hour (the best way), per diem, or a flat rate for the whole project, though it's best to use this latter method only for jobs you can do quickly and/or along with other jobs.[5]

For more information, see the articles cited here or look for courses on the subject. In New York City, courses have been offered at The New School, NYU in its School of Continuing Education, the Editorial Freelancers Association, and the International Center for Photography.

Research is the process of finding or verifying information to be used in the creation of a written work. Along the way you may have to do some fact checking, conduct interviews, and/or compile background information. Much of this work is ordinarily conducted by a writer or editor in the normal course of writing or editing a book or article, but occasionally writers, publishers, corporations, and packagers hire researchers to do this groundwork for them. Researchers charge by the hour, by the day, or by the project.

Rights and permissions refers to a highly specialized aspect of publishing that is only occasionally done on a freelance basis, and then only by people who are trained in the area. Anyone desiring to work in this field must first familiarize themselves with the laws governing copyrights. Basically, what's involved is searching out who owns the rights to various properties and then seeking their permission to use or quote from those properties in another work. In effect, a publisher would come to you with a book and ask you to determine everything that they need permission to use—quotations, cartoons, figures, tables, and so forth—and then write the copyright owners to secure their written permission to use the material. While this may sound straightforward, there are many gray areas, including the concept of "fair use." Sometimes determining who owns a particular work or finding the owner of a work is a problem. Still, you really do need to obtain permission in writing, because if material is published without securing such a permission and the owner later discovers this fact, the publisher can find itself facing a demand for an exorbitant fee or a suit for copyright infringement. Usually, however, getting permissions, including paying the fees, is the author's responsibility, not the publisher's. Working in rights and permissions can be time-consuming and frustrating and, in the long run, not very lucrative.

Translation is the process of rerendering a work in a different language, such as from Romanian into English. The work need not have been published, and the job can be as extensive as translating a book or as limited as checking someone else's translation of, say, figure captions for accuracy. A translator might be asked to provide other editorial services as well, such as copyediting or proofreading.

Word processing (keyboarding) is the process of taking copy, such as a book manuscript or newsletter article, and typing it onto a computer disk. This process can include imbedding computer typesetting codes, which are different from the specification code the copyeditor marks on the manuscript. For example, a copyeditor might put a circled capital A next to a first-level head, while a keyboarder would type something like <h1> next to the same head. The process of imbedding codes is very tedious and time-consuming, especially if you're coding a mathematics textbook, which involves a wide variety of codes. The possibility of creating errors is therefore much greater; for example, you might forget to type <p> at the beginning of a paragraph, or might type <p instead.

In 1987 the Association of American Publishers attempted to create a universal system—the Standard for Electronic Manuscript Preparation and Markup—but it didn't catch on. Consequently, there still is no standard set of typesetting codes that is used by all publishers and printers.

Although you may encounter other categories of editorial freelance work, for the most part they will be included in one of the broader areas covered in this chapter. In the next chapter we introduce some of the basic characteristics of an editorial freelancer, such as the freelance personality. Even if you're not new to editorial work or to freelancing, you may find some useful information in Chapters 2 and 3; if, on the other hand, you feel that the information will be too basic for you, you can skip to Chapter 4 or 5, where the discussion of the business of editorial freelancing per se begins.

NOTES

1. Christine Ammer, "Terms from Military History," *MHQ*, vol. 7, no. 1, Autumn 1994, p. 47.
2. "Editorial Style: Consistency Is the Aim," *The Editorial Eye*, Issue 48, Early October 1980, p. 1.
3. Nancy Evans, "Line editors: The rigorous pursuit of perfection," *Publishers Weekly*, October 15, 1979, p. 24.
4. William Bridgwater, "Copyediting," *Editors on Editing, What Writers Need to Know about What Editors Do*, Gerald Gross, Ed., Grosset Universal Library, New York, 1962; also 2nd ed., Harper & Row, New York, 1985.
5. Katherine A. Schmahl, "Picture Research," *EFA Newsletter*, vol. XIII, no. 2, November–December 1988, pp. 1, 4, 5.
6. Alice Lundoff, "The Picture Scene," *EFA Newsletter*, vol. XIII, no. 1, September–October 1988, p. 6.

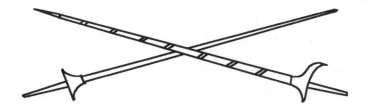

SETTING UP

People become editorial freelancers in two main ways: by choice or by circumstance. For example, there are those who take in-house editorial positions with the express purpose of gaining experience so they can later go freelance (choice); and those who have lost their jobs due to staff reductions, mergers, or other reorganization within a publishing house or business and need a haven until they can find another job (circumstance). Then there are those who lose their jobs, take freelance work to pay the bills, and find they like the lifestyle (choice plus circumstance). I'm sure we can all think of other examples, but these three illustrate the point.

Take those who choose to remain as freelancers. What is there about this profession that makes them realize that for them it's the best of all possible lifestyles? Besides the obvious answers, such as the fact that freelancers don't have to fight rush hour traffic on a daily basis or kowtow to ornery bosses, everybody has their own personalized list of reasons. Here are some of mine:

1. I work more comfortably when I can go at my own pace without someone looking over my shoulder.
2. I like being able to set my own schedules and the option of working as little or as much each day as I want.

3. I like the personal and professional freedom free-
    lancing affords me.
4. I thrive on solitude and quiet.
5. I enjoy the ambiance I've created in my workspace.

In items 1 through 4 we have begun to define what might be termed the "freelance personality."

THE FREELANCE PERSONALITY

Before you commit yourself to a career as an editorial freelancer, I strongly recommend that you engage in some honest self-analysis to determine whether you possess a personality that is suited to this way of life. Not having such a personality doesn't mean you can't succeed as a freelancer; it only suggests that you may not feel happy and ful-filled as a freelancer.

Briefly, a freelancer has to be able to work alone most of the time; to be disciplined enough to resist the call of the television set, the movie house, the sunny spring day, the afternoon bridge (or poker) game, and a multitude of other temptations in favor of meeting a deadline. Another thing to consider is that freelancers often have to convince their families and friends that just because they work at home doesn't mean they don't have a job or that their job isn't as important as that of someone who works in an office. (The way the world is turning these days, however, with increasing numbers of people, aided by technolo-gy such as modems and fax machines, going into business for them-selves, these latter considerations may soon no longer be valid.*) In fact, female freelancers are often viewed as choosing freelancing as a career "so they can stay home with their kids" rather than because they want to run a business. One woman I know told me that once at a social gathering she was asked what she did. When she answered, "I work at home," her interlocutor responded, "How wonderful that some people recognize the economic value of homemaking."

Freelancers also have to be able to live with uncertainty (where is the check for the job I finished a month ago? where will the next job come from?) as well as go that extra mile to complete a job on schedule when time grows short and the deadline looms large. In other words, they have to somehow arrange things so that they have sufficient quiet time

---

* In an article in *Publishers Weekly* ("Your Personal Bottom Line," April 25, 1994, p. 37), one chart indicates that, when asked "where they expected to be in five years," 15.1% of the 543 respondents said they thought they'd be self-employed.

to honor their obligations.

Which doesn't mean that the moment you don the mantle of "free-lancer" you have to give up all the other aspects of your life. In fact, whatever your circumstances, it's essential to your well-being that you make sure that you do have a life outside your job. As we'll see, the time a freelancer spends working is very focused because it isn't subject to the same interruptions and distractions that are usually encountered in an office. In fact, it has been said that for the freelancer the telephone sometimes acts as a substitute for office gossip. There will also be family emergencies and personal phone calls that will happen no matter the circumstances of your working life.

You also have to be able to say no to clients. I once knew an indexer who didn't get up until 2 P.M. because she preferred working during the quiet night hours. Unfortunately for her, most editors make calls in the morning, which meant that most of the time my friend was barely awake when she answered the phone. Not wanting to miss any opportunities, she'd say yes to every request, but because she wasn't very wide awake, she didn't keep track of her commitments from one call to the next. Later, and much to her chagrin, messengers would troop in like pageboys in a Peter Arno cartoon following a society matron after a morning's shopping, bearing one job after another. This is an extreme case, but it illustrates the point that it's easy to drown yourself with work if, like Ado Annie in "Oklahoma!," you cain't say no! As we'll see in Chapter 6, as a freelancer it's easy to get jammed up with work even if you pay close attention to scheduling.

And—very important!—you need to take periodic breaks. One colleague takes her dogs for a walk, another goes downstairs to get her mail or runs an errand in the neighborhood—whatever form your break may take, the brain doesn't need more than ten or fifteen minutes to refresh itself. It might be interesting to note that the physiological reason for this is that the brain needs a steady, available supply of glucose, and since it can't store it adequately, after a while it needs to be resupplied. When you take your break, you give your brain's blood supply an opportunity to restock itself with glucose. This is why the first half-hour of mental work is often the most productive.

Also, because our lives as freelancers are basically sedentary, it is essential to work an exercise program into your daily schedule. For example, I take yoga and do as much walking as I can. Both walking and swimming are excellent forms of exercise, the latter because so many muscles are involved. Or you can jog or play a sport like tennis or racquetball on a regular basis. If you decide to join a gym and work with weights and machines, look for one that has trainers who can familiarize you with the equipment, at least until you know enough about what you're doing so that you won't hurt yourself. Whatever form of exercise you decide on, I recommend choosing a program that exercises the cardiovascular system (unless your doctor forbids it). And remember, the slogan "No pain, no gain" may end in doing just that: putting you in pain, perhaps permanently.

It's also a fact of the freelance life that at the end of the day, one may feel like doing nothing more stimulating than collapsing in front of the television set or the VCR and vegetating. As a corollary, it is easy for freelancers who live alone to succumb to laziness, mainly because there is no one around to keep reminding them of their obligations. This is where discipline and the ability to make realistic schedules become so important. Without these attributes, freelancers often find themselves scurrying to catch up at the last minute. To avoid distraction, many freelancers, myself included, like to have several projects going at one time. In fact, the moment work slacks off, so do I, which makes it that much more difficult to gear up when work starts coming in again.

For those who live alone, it is easy to fall into a too-solitary lifestyle that can make one overly quirky and lonely. To avoid this unhealthy potential, it is essential to pay attention to one's aesthetic sense and social life. This can take the form of an occasional visit to a museum, a concert or theatrical subscription, a spur-of-the-moment movie, a walk in the park, lunches with friends, a night out with your spouse or significant other, watching your daughter's baseball game or your son's violin recital, and so on. This may seem to contradict what I said earlier about avoiding temptation, but it really isn't, because here I'm talking about activities outside of one's work time, which should include some relaxation and occasional spontaneity.

Once you've determined that you have the desire, self-discipline, and determination to make freelancing a way of life—that you'd enjoy and thrive on it—you're ready to proceed.

GOALS

Having made the decision to freelance, the first thing you need to do is sit down with a pad and pencil and write out your goals. At first glance this may seem like a task that should be put off until after one has learned a bit more about freelancing. Certainly, anyone who works alone is at high risk of becoming an accomplished procrastinator. So stay with this exercise until you've completed it. It will help you remain focused and on track both now and in the future.

As I said, before you can decide where to concentrate your energies, you need to establish your basic goals. To begin, there are four major areas to consider: the area of publishing you want to work in, the specialty or specialties you want to practice, the level of income you need in order to make freelancing viable, and the types of clients you want.

Although income needn't be the only consideration when determining the rest of your goals, it will probably be the primary one, so let's start with that.

Income

When considering income, the first question to ask yourself is why you've decided to become a freelancer. If it's to generate a second income for your family, you may not need to earn as much as you would if freelancing were going to be your only source of support. If that is the case, the amount you need to bring in may depend on the size of your family and the ages of your children. Another consideration is where you live. If you live in New York City, especially in Manhattan, your rent, food, and insurance costs will be higher than they would be in most other parts of the country, as will your taxes (for more on taxes, see Chapter 9)—yet at the same time your hourly rates will be lower (for more on rates, see Chapter 7).

Here are some other considerations that might make it easier for you to determine what you can reasonably expect to earn as a freelancer. If your dream is to work in mainstream publishing and you want to proofread for major publishers, you can expect to make no more than $15 per hour, except in unusual cases. On the other hand, proofreading for a bank or a large corporation can bring in as much as $40 per hour.

I'll say more about rates in Chapter 7. Meanwhile, to help you reach a realistic total, I'll cite a few figures from a survey published in 1994 by the Editorial Freelancers Association. The gross income for the 199 full-time freelancers who responded ranged from about $5000 to about $100,000 (I suspect this last was a lucky film script writer), with the largest percentage earning between $20,000 and $30,000.[1]

Area

There are four basic areas to be considered: mainstream publishing (which includes trade, textbook, professional, and reference); businesses, advertising agencies, and corporations; magazines; and professional journals. The one(s) you choose may depend on your financial needs, but let's suppose that you have a fairly clear idea of what you want your career path to look like. For me it was professional journals and mainstream publishing, because I'd been trained in the one and steeped in the other since birth.

If you envision a clientele similar to mine, bear in mind that you're unlikely to get rich. To quote from a short article of mine that appeared in *Publishers Weekly* in 1987: ". . . publishing must be the only industry in this country in which the rates paid their independent contractors—freelancers—have kept pace with neither the cost of living nor inflation."[2] In fairness, however, I should also point out that the profit margin in publishing is a lot less than it is in a corporation, which is one reason payments for services have remained low, although the tradition is rumored to have begun in the days when publishing had the reputation of being a gentleman's profession. In other words, one went into it, not because one needed to earn a living, but because one loved books and all things literary.

For those who don't want to earn the $9- to $40-per-hour rates that are standard in publishing, there are the higher paying corporate jobs where you can earn between $15 and $55 per hour for similar work. For a freelancer, however, working in-house for some businesses can be more stressful than working in-house for a publisher. All clients occasionally have emergencies, but some corporate jobs routinely include having someone "sitting on your shoulder" while you're working, incessantly asking how soon you'll be finished. Once, when working in-house for a consulting firm, I felt under more pressure during an average day than I do when doing an emergency project for a publisher.

Magazines and professional journals pay comparably to publishers, though finding work at the former can be difficult, as most of it is done by staff editors. Still, some magazines, such as *Time*, do hire freelance proofreaders—but again, the pressure can be very intense, especially when the time to "put it to bed"* draws closer.

Some subareas that you could also consider are newspapers, packagers† and total-concept houses, nonprofit organizations, the public sector (i.e., government agencies), and individuals (such as people looking for ghostwriters, students looking for someone to edit their dissertations, budding authors seeking to have their novels edited before submission to an agent or publisher).

---

* "Put it to bed" is jargon for sending the issue to the printer.

† Although they have some aspects in common with total-concept houses, packagers go further. They do everything from generating the idea to producing the finished product. They often need writers, copyeditors, proofreaders, picture researchers, designers, and, occasionally, factual researchers.

Specialty

The next thing to consider is the specialty or specialties you want to work in. Let me say here that the more you know about the publishing process, and the more skills you acquire, the more valuable you'll be to your clients. You can learn about the process of publishing a book by reading *Bookmaking* (Marshall Lee, Ed., Bowker, 1980); you can begin to learn new skills by taking courses (see Appendix C3). I say begin because you can never truly learn these skills until you practice them.

A case in point was cited by a former managing editor of St. Martin's Press. A certain freelancer was hired to read page proofs for a book. During the process, this individual made some changes that caused paragraphs to gain or lose lines. Being inexperienced with layout, the proofreader didn't realize the full effect of the changes: If the paragraphs lost or gained lines, then facing columns and/or pages would be uneven. The result was costly both in time and money, not to mention the freelancer's reputation. (In such a situation, if you see that a paragraph is going to gain or lose a line, you can compensate by either adding or deleting enough text to maintain the line count. If this is impossible, perhaps you can add or delete space around a head, list, displayed equation, or other design element. In any case, the change should be flagged for the client's approval.)

That said, let's consider some of your options, most of which were described briefly in Chapter 1: writer, editor, copyeditor, proofreader, indexer, researcher, picture researcher, translator. In making your decision, you might want to recall that corporations pay proofreaders $40 per hour and copyeditors $30 per hour, as opposed to the $12 and $15 per hour paid by most publishers for proofreading and copyediting, respectively.

Another aspect that you might want to consider is that writers and proofreaders are used more frequently in the corporate/business world than editors/copyeditors. There are two reasons for this: (1) editing in a corporation is usually done by a staff editor, and (2) proofreaders often function as copyeditors. Therefore, if you want to do copyediting for corporations, it might be safer to call yourself a proofreader.

One caveat that needs to be made here is that the corporate world doesn't make the same fine distinctions that the publishing world does. For example, to a corporate client *editor* means someone who can do everything from substantive editing to the most basic copyediting. Also, in the corporate world writers are considered to be more on the same level as consultants and are therefore given more autonomy than, say, editors. On the other hand, although they are well paid, proofreaders are considered to occupy a fairly low level, which means that they are more at the mercy of the company in that work can be dropped in their lap at the last minute without any warning and wanted back within a day or two. The upside of all this is that if you've established a long-term working relationship with a small company doing, say, the lowest level of editing (i.e., copyediting), there is a good chance you'll be given the opportunity to develop new marketable skills—for example, in the production end of things. For more on freelancing in the corporate world, see Chapter 5.

In another area, some professional journals prefer a freelancer who can take an issue all the way through the editorial process and supply administrative backup (maintaining files, sending faxes and letters, trafficking, etc.) as well. Others follow the tradition in which the person who copyedits a piece shouldn't proofread it, the idea being that if you make a mistake during the former stage, you'll likely perpetuate it during the latter.

Types of Clients

The types of clients you choose to work for will depend largely on the area in which you want to work. For example, if you want to proofread annual reports for corporations, you shouldn't be approaching small print shops. Of course, when you're getting started you might occasionally look for a lower paying client to help pay the rent (we talk more about this in Chapter 7), but such a client shouldn't be on your list of goals. For more on good freelance business practices, see Chapter 6.

Of course not all corporations are equal, by which I mean that not all companies in this category pay the same rates. For example, some large pharmaceutical companies pay rates that are fairly comparable to those paid by publishers.

Following are lists of some of the types of clients in the two main categories mentioned earlier. These are by no means complete listings; you should always be on the lookout for new clients of any stripe.

Mainstream publishing: trade houses, textbook houses (both el-hi* and college), lawbook publishers, packagers and total-concept houses, professional publishers, reference publishers, juvenile publishers, university presses, university offices of advertising and publications services, and last but not least, the small print shop.

Corporations: advertising agencies, consulting firms, nonprofit associations, professional associations, foundations, accounting and management consulting firms, law offices, and public relations firms.

While mainstream publishers produce mostly traditional and interactive books (such as encyclopedias, which are on CD-ROM [compact

---

*Producers of elementary and high school instructional materials.

disc read-only memory]), corporations and businesses generate the following types of publications, among others: annual reports, newsletters and house organs, corporate periodicals, manuals and other forms of documentation, handbooks and monographs, business proposals, press releases, promotional pieces and brochures, advertising copy, audiovisual materials, and catalogs. (Of course publishing companies also produce many of these items, but whether they pay as well as corporations is another question.)

Reviewing Your Goals

Now that you've focused on your goals, review them before filing them away. For example, suppose that you've decided you want an income of $40,000; you want to work as a proofreader; you want to establish yourself in the world of corporate proofreading; and you want to work for advertising agencies, popular news magazines, and law firms. Now let's throw in one more goal: to be the best in your field.

Although you're putting your list of goals in a drawer, don't let them just lie there. Take them out every few months and assess your progress. This is also a good time to reconsider your goals. If you find that one of them is no longer valid, get rid of it and replace it. This process will help you redefine your career as it shifts and grows.

Before we can explore ways to approach the clients on your list of goals, or find other ones, we need to take some time to consider your workspace and the books and other supplies you'll need in order to function effectively as an editorial freelancer. These matters are discussed in the next chapter.

NOTES

1. *Editorial Freelancers Association Professional Practices Survey,* Editorial Freelancers Association, New York, 1994.
2. Trumbull Rogers, "On the Road to Mediocrity," *Publishers Weekly,* December 4, 1987, p. 42.

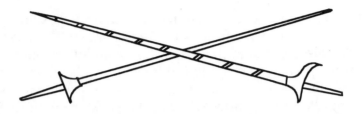

THE FREELANCER'S OFFICE

3

I think we can all agree that it takes more than the accoutrements of an editorial professional to make one an editor. Still, there's a fine line here, because a person cannot function as an editorial freelancer without the proper equipment. Speaking for a moment to the newcomer, in all likelihood you already own a great many of these items, but once you start using them professionally, they will take on a new significance. Being a frugal person, unfortunately I once got upset at my young grandson when he wasted some of my Scotch tape and took my colored pencils to play with, both natural acts for a boy his age. I suspect you will become equally possessive of *your* scissors, *your* dictionary, *your* ruler when they are not ready to hand when you need them.

For the purposes of this book we'll refer to the place where you do your freelance work as an office. But it likely won't be an office in the most typical sense of the word. For one thing, it will doubtless become a highly personalized place. For another, physically it can be as small "as a postage stamp" or as grand as a room on its own. Whatever the case, in this chapter we review some of the tools and treasures you will need to collect and maintain there.

THE WORKSPACE

As you can imagine, an editorial freelancer has the flexibility to work in an "office" of any size, from a cleared space on the dining room table, to a corner of a room that has been made into a work area, to a separate room. I knew one successful freelancer who always appeared to work on the couch in her living room, another who works in bed, another who likes to sit under a tree in the park, one who prefers her front porch, and another who works on her kitchen table. In my last New York apartment, I had a portion of my living room partitioned off by bookcases. It doesn't matter how big or elaborate your workspace is, it only matters that it is a place where you consistently do your work. I don't recommend, however, that you use your bedroom, because you'll likely end up feeling closed in, as your entire life will seem to be spent between the same four walls. In my first New York apartment, where the bathroom was larger than the kitchen and the bedroom probably wouldn't have qualified under the terms of the Geneva Convention, I made a vow that my next apartment would be large enough so that when I went from one room to another I would feel as though I had gone somewhere.

Of course not every freelancer is going to be able to afford the luxury of living in an apartment larger than a studio. Many have therefore devised strategies to counteract the mind-numbing effects of living and working in the same small space. Some examples might be starting the day with a workout at the local gym; going for a long walk before work, especially for dog owners; or going out to breakfast, which can have the effect of giving a sense of then "coming to the office."

In one of the sessions of my course on launching a freelance business, a student asked if I had any suggestions on how to choose furniture so that one would be most comfortable while sitting for hours at a time. The first thing I'd say on that subject is this: because your surroundings are so important to your relaxation and concentration, you should arrange them so that you are both physically and psychologically supported. For this reason, the two most important items in your office will be the desk you work at and the chair you sit in.

Since you'll spend a great deal of time in it, you should put a lot of thought into choosing your chair. The bad news is that most chairs aren't designed to be sat in, but to look nice. A chiropractor once told me that most back pain is caused by the chairs we sit in and how we sit in them. (Some of the worst offenders are the seats in automobiles, movie theaters, concert halls, sports arenas, subway cars, and buses.) One way to attain a relaxed, upright posture in a chair is to push your bottom as far back on the seat as you can. Then, with your feet placed flat on the floor, open your knees until they are outside the edges of the chair. If your shoulders are still rounded forward and your chest slightly concave, lift your thoracic area gently until your spine is fully extended. To make this position viable, of course, you need to place yourself at the best distance from your desk to see and work on the manuscript or galleys comfortably.

Finding the perfect chair will take some time and experimentation. When you go shopping for a chair, spend some time sitting in it before you decide to buy it. Does it support your back and lower spine? Does it make you want to sit up straight? Or does it encourage you to slouch? Does it fit you? For instance, do your feet rest comfortably on the floor? Will your legs fit comfortably under your desk when you're seated in it? But most important, do you feel at ease sitting in it? First think about these factors. Then think about appearance and color.

Choosing a desk is a bit more tricky. The reason is that when you lay a manuscript on a flat surface to read it, your head will naturally incline forward. Since your head weighs about twenty pounds, this position puts a terrific strain on your cervical vertebrae. As a result you can develop pain and stiffness, primarily in the neck, the thoracic area of the back, and the trapezius and interrelated muscles. Headaches and fatigue may result.

To counteract this situation, I adopted a setup used by an editor at one of my clients' offices. It consisted of a large piece of plywood about a half inch thick laid against an artist's table easel, adjusted to a comfortable angle (20 degrees is usually recommended). The sheets of the manuscript were held by two legal size clipboards that lay side by side on the plywood board. The lower tray of the easel formed a stop for the bottoms of the clipboards, as well as serving as a place to lay a pencil. Other important papers were held by large stainless clips at the top of the board. In an artist's supply store I found a pencil cup that attached with a clamp to the board. Over time, however, the easel began to give way (probably because the board was too wide and too heavy for it), so I was constantly leaning on one side of the board to keep it from tilting while writing on it.

When considering whether to adopt this or one of the following options, or none of them, remember that you'll want to have enough space left over for your computer, printer, and/or fax. In most of the arrangements described here, however, such an option may not be feasible, in which case you'll need a separate computer table.

I finally found salvation in a catalog. It is a desk made of tulip wood that may have been designed for an architect or other draftsman, but is also perfect for an editor or proofreader (see Figure 1). All I had to do was add a lip to hold my clipboards and replace the flimsy wooden pegs that supported the desk's lift top with steel bolts. Although I have never seen this particular desk advertised again, I'm sure any competent cabinetmaker could build a reasonable facsimile of the one just described. Also it's possible that investing some time in a little detective work could unearth a desk of a similarly satisfactory design.

Associate Editor Richard Stiefel, who works in the editorial offices of another of my clients, has found a system that he swears by. Called Editor's Desk, it can be purchased from the Levenger catalog. It comes in two sizes and four colors. The large size is twenty-five inches wide by fourteen inches deep, and the medium size is eighteen inches wide by fourteen inches deep. Richard has the latter size, and finds it just right for his purposes. The work surface is a board set at a comfortable, though unadjustable, angle that sits on the desk. It has a lip to hold the bottom edge of your papers, and two sheets can lie side by side. There is even a grooved tray for pencils and it has an upper shelf that will hold a desk dictionary or other reference book. Transparent writing pads are available for both models. While you're at it, you might want to check out the Portable Editor's Desk in the same catalog. It's made of birch wood and is 13¾ inches by 18 inches. For a few extra dollars you can buy a carry bag for it.

Such devices allow you to work with your head upright, which relieves your neck of extra strain and helps you avoid tiring easily. If, however, you opt for the more traditional flat-top desk, be sure it's large enough to accommodate all of your paraphernalia. If you choose an angled desk top, be sure to provide adequate flat surfaces on both sides for turned pages and to hold such things as a pencil sharpener, stapler, and telephone (see figure).

The next consideration is light. Besides the overhead light in the room, I have a Tensor lamp above my desk to provide extra illumination. I don't necessarily recommend this system, but whatever setup you adopt, be sure the light doesn't shine in your eyes, and that your work is bathed in adequate light that casts no distracting shadows. I prefer Soft White bulbs to reduce the glare. On the other hand, I've been told that fluorescent light is probably the worst on your eyes and for your health. If you use a pole or floor lamp, the best location is behind your left shoulder (or right, if you're left-handed), but since that's not always practical, try to position it so glare and shadows are minimized.

Other necessary items of furniture are file cabinets, bookcases, and a computer table. My first file cabinets were two-drawer wooden ones,

Figure 1. The author's desk. Note the shelf for reference books above the desk's adjustable slanted work surface; the large metal clips, the left one holding a time sheet; the pencil cup on the extreme right; the lip holding two clipboards with manuscript attached and dictionary; the space for reference books on the left and drawer for supplies on the right; and the flat surfaces on either side created by two-drawer file cabinets.

Photo: Martha Solonche

but file cabinets fill up fast. It might therefore be better to start with a four-drawer model. I bought mine second-hand from the Salvation Army, but you can find them at used office furniture stores as well. They can also be purchased from office supply stores and some department stores. If you buy a used one, a fresh coat of paint will brighten it up. If space is limited, you might be able to locate it in a closet.

Bookcases can be of several varieties. I prefer the tension pole type so I can have my reference library over my desk. Similar to this is the kind built from metal strips that are attached to the wall by toggle bolts. These strips hold brackets on which the shelves lie. Not all walls will take toggle bolts, however, so you may have to use plugs.* If you do, I recommend that you not use the plastic ones, because chances are the bookcase will have to support a heavy weight, and I've seen bookcases anchored in this fashion pull out of the wall. Some of the metal plugs available today should be adequate for the purpose, however. If you can afford it, built-in bookcases are probably the best because you can design them to fit your workspace and they're the most sturdily built. Otherwise the ready-made, unpainted variety are perfectly adequate.

If you need a separate table for your computer, the first thing to know is that it's not necessary to buy a table that has been designed specifically for that purpose. I use what would today be called a sofa table, but which in its day functioned more as a kind of occasional table in the living room of the house where I was born. Since it is wide and deep enough to hold my computer, mouse pad, printer, disks, some books, the papers I'm working from, a small ceramic statue of Groucho Marx, my coffee mug, and has drawers for supplies, I long ago adapted it for use—first as my desk, and more recently as my computer table. All of which is to say that you can use almost any table, as long as it's large enough to hold the important items just listed. If you're taking a home office deduction and/or are deducting the cost of your computer as a business expense, the IRS insists that the computer be located in your work area and that it be dedicated exclusively to business-related activities.

Whatever your workspace looks like, you'll need a place to store office supplies. Depending on your situation, this can be as large as a separate cabinet or as small as a shelf in a closet or a drawer in your desk. I store very little in my desk drawers because that's where I keep supplies for current use—paper clips, pencils, rubber bands, Post-its,

---

* In this instance, the word *plugs* refers to the plastic or metal sheaths that are inserted into holes drilled in the wall, and which then hold the screws that attach the metal strips to the wall.

paper, Scotch tape, and so forth. Whatever storage system you choose should be handy, yet off limits to foraging family members.

As a final touch, you may want to hang a favorite picture where you can see it when you glance up from work, and/or scatter some favorite knickknacks or objets d'art nearby. This way you'll feel that you are working in a familiar and comfortable environment.

One problem shared by many freelancers is the unfettered growth of objects in their offices. For example, one freelancer I know routinely accumulates the following stuff: books, photos, knickknacks, souvenirs, supplies, job folders, notes to herself, tapes for her tape player, birdseed for her window feeder, calendars, computer disks, to cite the short list. I have a similar pack-rat instinct, and find the mounds of papers, etc., somehow comforting—to a point. When I begin to feel overwhelmed I take a few minutes to organize: filing papers, notes, and newsletters; putting magazines in their proper piles and throwing some away; rearranging some of the piles; moving some things to their proper locations in the apartment. I even had two seed packets (one for forget-me-nots and one for cabbage); I gave away the flowers, but no one wanted the cabbage, so after about two years I threw out the packet. Obviously I'm not a person who discards stuff easily. That is my solution to the problem of "clutter"; you may find that you need to develop one of your own. Or, if that doesn't work, you can either buy one of the myriad books on organizing or hire a professional organizer to help you straighten things out.

BASIC EQUIPMENT

When you set up an editorial freelancing business, you will want to be sure that you have the following basic equipment (see also Figure 2). Some of it is so obvious, I won't discuss it; some of it is discussed in depth elsewhere in this book (see chapter citations); and some of it will be described briefly here.

Fax machine: When I first began presenting my course in 1991, the fax was at the bottom of this list. Now people no longer ask if you have a fax; they ask for your fax number. While it might not be so important for copyeditors to have one, a fax is essential for development editors and writers. Still, as an editor I'm asked if I have one often enough to make it worth the expense. Most business experts recommend that you should have a separate phone line for it, but if you can't afford both a second line and a fax, you can get along with a single line.

1. Fax machine
2. Telephone, number, and line for business calls
3. Computer (486; IBM compatible)
4. Telephone answering machine
5. Printer ribbons or cartridges
6. Number 2 lead pencils
7. Col-erase pencils
   (a) blue (#1276)
   (b) brown (#1272)
   (c) carmine red (#1277)
   (d) green (#1278)
8. Pica ruler
9. Window and wheel
10. Pens
11. Paper clips
12. Scotch tape
13. White out
    (a) Liquid Paper (black)
    (b) Pen & Ink (green)
    (c) Just for Copies (red)
14. Stapler, staples, and staple remover
15. Post-its
16. Editorial flags (usually Post-its are used for this function)
17. Correction tape
18. Scissors
19. Mailing labels
20. Letterhead stationery and matching envelopes
21. Computer and fax paper
22. 20-lb bond
23. File folders
24. Large mailing envelopes (for returning mss.)
25. Business cards
26. Diary and Work Log
27. Tape recorder (for writers)

Figure 2. Basic equipment.

Telephone, number, and line for business calls: If you don't want to pay for Speed Calling or an equivalent, I suggest you get a model that includes a memory feature so you can dial your clients by pressing a single button. As with the fax, you should have a separate business line. Besides being more professional, it helps keep your business calls separate from your personal ones, which makes it easier to identify them come tax time. If you don't want to do this, then I'd recommend getting Call Waiting—not a bad idea for the business line, if you do get one—so that family members can let you take business calls when they come in.

Computer (486; IBM compatible) and printer: These are discussed in Chapter 4.

Telephone answering machine: Next to the phone, fax, and computer, this is the most important piece of equipment in your office. One vital feature shared by virtually every model is a remote call-in system that allows you to check your messages from other locations. I say vital because this may be the only way you can find out about potential jobs in a timely manner. Fortunately, since you can't have both a fax and an answering machine attached to the same phone, many faxes come with an answering machine installed.

Printer ribbons or cartridges, depending on the type of printer you have.

Number 2 lead pencils: These head the list because they are the most popular type of pencil used by editors. The lead is just the right weight so that it marks clearly without smudging. It is also the most easily photocopied of any of the colors.

Col-erase pencils:

(a) *Blue (#1276):* Although the blue pencil is still very much associated with editing and has even come into the language (according to *Merriam Webster's Collegiate Dictionary* [Tenth Edition], **blue-pencil** (vt) means "to edit esp. by shortening or deletion"), it is rarely used by editors anymore for the simple reason that it does not photocopy. Because of this I use mine mostly to mark instructions on line art and other items that I don't want to be picked up* by the photographing process.

(b) *Brown (#1272):* This is a soft, restful color, and is easily photocopied. I have seen it used mainly by math editors, but it may have lost favor because the vividness of the color became unpredictable—sometimes too light; sometimes just right.

(c) *Carmine red (#1277):* Much used by editors because it stands out and photocopies well. Carmine is the shade most preferred, a fact it took me a while to learn after I started freelancing. Its one major disadvantage is that it's also the color used by teachers to grade papers. This fact sometimes causes authors to react adversely, so some editors use other, friendlier colors such as green.

(d) *Green (#1278):* Also a popular color with editors for the same reasons red is. The last time I used it, however, I found that it came off on my fingers. If you find you have a problem like this with any of these colored pencils, Col-erase representatives are very responsive and will try to get the fault corrected if they can.

A pica† ruler: Since the pica is the basic unit of measure in bookmaking, the pica ruler can be considered to be as basic a tool as the pencil. My first pica ruler was transparent, which came in handy because I was doing layout as well as editing at the time. The clear plastic type

---

* Here "picked up" means that the photographic process will record the mark in question. Thus, if I want to show the compositor where to place the "(a)"s and "(b)"s on a piece of art without the instruction being "picked up," I use a blue pencil because the marks won't be recorded by the camera.

† One pica equals about 1/6 of an inch, or 12-point type.

can also be useful in proofreading when you need to check the space around heads, lists, or other displayed material. Now, however, I prefer my steel model, which has the inch scale on the edge opposite the pica scale, making it easy to convert picas to inches (and vice versa) when necessary. Although this model comes in plastic as well, I find the steel version to be more durable.

Window and proportion wheel: These items are essential for figuring reduction of photographs and line art. Figure reduction is a good skill for any editor to have, especially if you're working on journal articles, where you're apt to be required to work on the figures; in books the art program is usually handled by the art department. The reason for reducing figures is that the text portion of books and magazine articles is set at a certain width and depth, say twenty-seven picas by forty-three picas, and the figures and their captions have to fit within these parameters. At the same time, any type that appears on the art has to be large enough to be easily read—eight point is preferred, and certainly no smaller than six point. The window is a piece of clear plastic with the various type sizes on it. By laying it on the lettering on a piece of line art or combination cut,* you can determine the point size of the type. Some editors use the Haberule for this purpose, but I think it's easier to judge typesize with a window. The wheel helps you find the percentage of reduction and tells you whether reducing the art by that amount will still allow the figure labels to be read. You should be able to find both the window and wheel at any reasonably stocked art supply store. Some stationery stores also carry them.

Pens: I use pens mainly for recordkeeping. Some editors edit in ink, and McGraw-Hill prefers that their editors use green ink, but, like most editors, I find myself changing my mind about points of style too often to be comfortable editing in ink. And I've known of situations where editors have lost potential clients because they insisted on editing with a pen. There are times, however, when I will use a pen—for example, for manuscript coding, because some colored inks stand out more clearly than comparable pencil colors.

Paper and binder clips: You should keep a supply of medium and large paper clips, as well as small, medium, and large binder clips, on hand so you're prepared for any size manuscript (never staple manuscript pages together).

Scotch tape: Although I prefer three-quarter-inch Scotch Magic Tape, almost any transparent tape that can be written on is okay.

---

*A combination cut is a photograph (halftone) with type superimposed on it.

White out: I prefer Liquid Paper, because it comes in several handy varieties:

(a) Liquid Paper (black label) for most corrections.

(b) Pen & Ink (green label) because the underlying ink doesn't leach through and because you can write on it after it's dried, features the standard Liquid Paper lacks.

(c) Just for Copies (red label) for corrections on photocopies, which tend to smear when the other varieties are applied.

Stapler, staples, and staple remover.

Post-its in various sizes: 1½″ x 2″; 3″ x 3″; and 3″ by 5″ should suffice.

Editorial flags: Since Post-its are generally used for this purpose these days, if the traditional 2¼″ x 6″ gummed type are requested, ask the in-house editor to send along a supply with the project.

White correction tape of various widths, particularly one-line and two-line.

Scissors.

Gummed mailing labels (e.g., 1¾″ x 4¹⁄₁₆″) to affix to the packages you send back to your clients. Or, if you can set up your computer for it, use the self-sticking variety you find on much of your mail.

Letterhead stationery and matching envelopes: You may want the stationery in note-pad size as well as letter size. These can be bought at either a stationery/office supply store or a photocopy shop. In either case, you will be offered a choice of typefaces; avoid fancy script and italic faces as they do not appear businesslike. You can also include your logo, if you have one, but you'll have to supply them with camera-ready copy.

Computer and fax paper: For the majority of uses, I find that 20-lb photocopy paper is sufficient for printer uses. As for the fax, paper is now available that can be used by all faxes.

20-lb bond: This comes in handy for printing manuscripts, as well as bills and other items that you want to look their best.

File folders: I prefer the straight-cut style, but you may find that you like the third cut assorted tab style better. This is one of those subjective choices where one style is neither superior nor inferior to the other.

Large envelopes: A supply of 6 by 9, 10 by 13, and 14 by 19½ envelopes should be fine for most uses. If larger or smaller ones are required, you can purchase them at your stationery store. I also keep on hand a supply of Federal Express and Express and Priority Mail envelopes as well as labels for all three kinds on hand.

Business cards: These are discussed in Chapter 5, but for where to buy, etc., see the earlier discussion under "Letterhead stationery and matching envelopes."

Diary and Work Log: These, along with the daily expense record, are discussed in Chapter 6.

A tape recorder: Handy for recording interviews or stories, if you're a writer.

THE FREELANCER'S BASIC LIBRARY

The books listed and discussed in this section make up my ideal of the freelance editor's basic library (for more books of interest to freelancers, see Appendic C1). Talk to other freelancers, and they'll have other ideas, especially on specific titles,* but I don't think the differences will be that great. The entire list appears in Figure 3, so you can easily refer to it. The first eight books are the absolute minimum; the first twelve the ideal minimum. I've added the rest to give you some ideas for rounding out your collection.

Reference books are quite expensive, but they can sometimes be found in used-book stores. Some of the larger chains, such as Barnes & Noble, may offer some at a discount, so it's a good idea to shop around for the best price. I started collecting my library at Strand Book Store, a used-book emporium in New York that has a large reference section. A diligent search of the titles yielded me some recent editions, and some fun titles as well. A case in point is a slim volume titled *A Comparative Study of Spellings.* Until I discovered this book I never knew that different dictionaries spell the same words differently. The four dictionaries compared were *The Random House Dictionary of the American Language, College Edition* (1969), *Webster's Seventh New Collegiate Dictionary* (1969), *Webster's New World Dictionary of the American Language* (1970), and *The American Heritage Dictionary of the English Language* (1969). One example: At that time Random House's and American Heritage's Collegiate Dictionaries gave *farm hand* as the preferred spelling, while Webster and New World gave *farmhand.* Other differences could be seen in hyphenation and the treatment of variants, such as *flustration* and *flusteration* or *footsie* and *footsy.*

In some instances—for example, Bartlett's and Roget's— you can buy a used older edition and then get a more recent edition when you can afford it. Others, like numbers 1, 2, 4, and 5, really should be the most recent editions.

Also be warned that some of these books may have to be ordered,

---

* For example, see Martin Kohl, *The Freelancer's Bookshelf,* Editorial Freelancers Association, New York, 1994.

Basic Reference Library
1. *Webster's Tenth New Collegiate Dictionary*
2. *Chicago Manual of Style* (14th Edition)
3. An up-to-date encyclopedia (Columbia, 5/e; or desk)
4. *Webster's Biographical Dictionary*
5. *Webster's New Geographical Dictionary* (or a good atlas)
6. *World* (or comparable) *Almanac*
7. *Roget's Thesaurus* (5/e)
8. *Bartlett's Familiar Quotations*

Additional Useful References
9. An unabridged dictionary, preferably *Webster's Third New International Dictionary* (Merriam-Webster)
10. A dictionary of the specialty area in which you work; e.g., medical (*Dorland's Medical Dictionary* (27/e))
11. A style book for the specialty area in which you work; e.g., psychology (APA style book—good to have in case a client wants references done in that style)
12. *Fowler's Modern English Usage* and/or a good grammar book (e.g., Strunk and White's *The Elements of Style*)

Other Useful Books
13. Your client's style manual or other styling materials
14. Foreign language dictionaries
15. *Words into Type*
16. Other books you feel will be helpful. Some of my favorites are:
    (a) *The Random House Webster's Spell Checker,* which I prefer to *20,000 Words* (for word breaks)
    (b) *The Handbook of Nonsexist Writing* (2/e), Casey Miller and Kate Swift (HarperCollins)
    (c) An abbreviations/acronyms dictionary
    (d) A computer dictionary; e.g., I like *The Random House Personal Computer Dictionary* (new and comprehensive) or *Microsoft Press Computer Dictionary* (2/e)
    (e) ZIP codes book
    (f) *The McGraw-Hill Style Manual,* Marie M. Longyear, Ed.
    (g) *Chicago Guide to Preparing Electronic Manuscripts* (University of Chicago Press, 1987)
    (h) *The Encyclopedia of American Facts and Dates* (9/e), Gorton Carruth, Ed. (HarperCollins, 1993)
    (i) A movie and video guide (I like Leonard Maltin's)
    (j) A guide to television programs

Some Style Manuals
17. *Manual of Style* (8/e)—American Medical Association (AMA)
18. *Scientific Style and Format* (6/e) (Cambridge/Council of Biology Editors)
19. *ACS Style Guide* (American Chemical Society)
20. *Publication Manual of the American Psychological Assn.* (3/e)
21. *Mathematics into Type* (Rev. Ed.) (American Mathematical Society)
22. *Style Manual* (3/e) (American Institute of Physics)

Figure 3. Recommended basic reference library.

since not all bookstores stock them. If yours charges a fee for taking special orders, you can call the publisher directly and order it yourself.

Basic Reference Library

1. *Webster's Tenth New Collegiate Dictionary:* Webster's is the most preferred desk dictionary in the publishing industry. Only once in my twenty years of freelancing have I been asked to use another dictionary (the New World). The one thing I miss in the Tenth is the list of colleges that the Ninth and older editions included in their back matter.

2. *Chicago Manual of Style* (14th edition): Most publishing houses have their own style manuals, some more complete than others. All other style questions are settled by reference to *Chicago,* sometimes referred to as the Bible of copyediting. It is the closest thing the publishing industry has to a standard style manual, so you should familiarize yourself with it, particularly Part Two on style.

3. An up-to-date encyclopedia. I prefer *The Columbia Encyclopedia* (fifth edition), but there are also good desk encyclopedias, such as *Webster's New World Encyclopedia* (College Edition) (Prentice Hall, 1993) and the *Cambridge Paperback Encyclopedia* (Cambridge University Press, 1993), that will be adequate to your purpose.

4. *Webster's Biographical Dictionary.* Probably one of the best of its kind, although it gives original spellings of names. This is always the first place I go to check birth and death dates. These won't always agree with the dates the author gives, so if it's only a year or two off, check another source, like the encyclopedia. The author may have used still another source, so point out the discrepancy, name the books you've consulted, and leave it up to him or her to make the final decision.

5. *Webster's New Geographical Dictionary.* I find this book easier to use than an atlas. It lists cities, towns, countries, and topographical features in alphabetical order and gives some statistics about each entry. With the world changing as fast as it does, expect even the latest edition to be out of date—the same as any atlas.

6. An almanac. Essential for checking some statistics and spellings, especially the names of large corporations, politicians, and media celebrities.

7. *Roget's Thesaurus* (fifth edition). I name this one because I prefer it, but there are other good thesauruses. This book comes in very handy when you want to find the word that most closely conveys the author's meaning, or when you want to find a word that better connotes the meaning a non-native English speaker is trying to express.

8. *Bartlett's Familiar Quotations.* This is good for checking quotations,

bits of verse, and epigraphs. My only problem with this type of book is that newer editions drop some useful quotes to make room for more contemporary ones. This is unavoidable, but it does become annoying when I want to check a quotation that I know was in the last edition, only to find it absent from the current one.

Additional Useful References

9. An unabridged dictionary. The standard for the publishing industry is *Webster's Third New International Dictionary.* Be sure the publisher is Merriam-Webster, the company that holds the copyright for the Webster's imprint. Barnes & Noble in New York sells a knock-off unabridged dictionary called *Webster's New Universal Unabridged Dictionary* for about $30, but this is no more the real McCoy than are the five dollar dictionaries sold by street vendors. (These latter are printed from old plates, say the 1930s or 1940s, which makes them horribly out of date.)

10. A dictionary for the specialty area within which you work; for example, for medical editing, you should consider either *Dorland's Medical Dictionary* (twenty-seventh edition) (Saunders) or *Stedman's Medical Dictionary* (twenty-fifth edition, 1990), but if you only need a general reference, *Mosby's Medical and Nursing Dictionary* (second edition) is often recommended.

11. A style book for the specialty area in which you work; for example, the APA style manual if you're specializing in psychology. This particular manual is handy to have in any case, because you may sometimes be asked to style references according to APA style.

12. *Fowler's Modern English Usage* (second edition) and/or a good grammar book. *Fowler* is still the standard for settling sticky questions of grammar and usage, having survived the one major criticism I've ever heard about it—that it's *English* usage, not American. If this bothers you, then perhaps you should take a look at Wilson Follett's *Modern American Usage* (Hill & Wang, 1966), Roy H. Copperud's *American Usage and Style: The Consensus* (Van Nostrand Reinhold, 1979), or Theodore Bernstein's *The Careful Writer: A Modern Guide to English Usage* (Atheneum, 1977). Once the assistant managing editor of the *New York Times,* Bernstein was widely known in the industry for his bulletin on better writing, called *Winners & Sinners,* which was circulated to reporters and editors.

Usage questions can also be answered by the dictionary, or you can try *The McGraw-Hill Style Manual* (see below). A friend and long-time editor once told me she rereads Strunk and White's *The Elements of*

Style once a year in order to refresh her knowledge of grammar. This is probably one of the best grammar books around—certainly one of the shortest—and probably the most popular, though another good one to consider is James Fernald's *English Grammar Simplified.*

Other Useful Books

13. Your client's style manual or other styling materials. I've been collecting these for as long as I've been freelancing. Although the style manual of the Institute of Electrical and Electronics Engineers has probably been updated since I left there in 1975, I still find some of its sections indispensable. Usually these manuals will be supplied with your first job, along with a separate set of instructions, some of which may deviate from the house's standard style. These deviations might result from an author's insistence that "data" be construed as singular or from an in-house decision that all tables retain their vertical rules.

14. Foreign language dictionaries, especially French and Spanish. The ones you should get depend on the type of work you're doing. If you're editing a lot of medical material, a Latin dictionary (and grammar) might come in handy. For psychology, you may want a German dictionary. I also find occasional use for an Italian dictionary.

15. *Words into Type,* by Marjorie E. Skillin and Robert M. Gay. This is another often-mentioned style manual. In the twenty years that I've been freelancing, however, I've been specifically asked to use it only twice. Still, I know some freelancers who prefer it to *Chicago,* and others who like it for some of its sections—for example, it provides information on grammar and usage, which *Chicago* does not—so it would make a good addition to your library. (N.B.: As I write this, *Words into Type* is being revised for publication in 1995, though it could be out as early as late summer 1994.)

16. Here are a couple of books that might be helpful. They aren't all included in the figure, but you might enjoy knowing about them.

(a) A spell checker. I prefer *The Random House Webster's Spell Checker* because it has more entries than *20,000 Words.* Its only drawback is that because it's a vest pocket dictionary, the typesize is quite small. These spell checkers are handy for checking word breaks, and I find them easier to use than a dictionary when I need to check spelling while I'm working at my computer.

(b) *The Handbook of Nonsexist Writing* (second edition), by Casey Miller and Kate Swift (HarperCollins, 1988). This handy little book is very helpful in supplying alternative words for sexist language. The first book of this type—and probably the model for all subsequent ones—was *Guidelines for Bias-Free Publishing* (McGraw-Hill), but it may not be too easy to get ahold of unless you do work for McGraw.

(c) A dictionary of abbreviations and acronyms. I use several lists that I've collected over the years, and *Webster's Tenth* also contains a list of abbreviations, but the one that often comes through in a pinch is Ralph De Sola's *Abbreviations Dictionary* (eighth edition) (CRC Press, 1992).

(d) A computer dictionary. I like *The Random House Personal Computer Dictionary* because it's as up-to-date as any computer dictionary can be and is written in clear, comprehensible language. You might also want to check out the *IBM Dictionary of Computing* (18,000 entries) (McGraw-Hill, 1994) or the *Microsoft Press Computer Dictionary* (second edition) (Microsoft Press, 1994). But if all you want is a good, basic dictionary, Kent Porter's *The New American Computer Dictionary* (NAL-Dutton, 1983) is a good one to consider.

(e) A ZIP codes book. I find this a useful book, especially when authors don't include ZIP codes in their addresses or to find the correct spelling of hospital or street names. The U.S. Postal Service sells its edition for $15, but you can find less expensive ones in most bookstores.

(f) *The McGraw-Hill Style Manual,* Marie M. Longyear, Ed. (McGraw-Hill, 1989). I find this book particularly useful for looking up questions of usage. This section is alphabetized and covers words whose meanings are often confused, such as *comprise* and *compose.* To a great extent, in matters of grammar and style, it parallels McGraw's in-house style book, *Editing and Composition Standards* (ECS). Since McGraw's style is the basis for the styles of several other houses, I find Longyear's book very handy to have.

(g) *Chicago Guide to Preparing Electronic Manuscripts for Authors and Publishers* (University of Chicago Press, 1987). With systems such as PenEdit (see Chapter 4) coming on the market, this little book may become obsolete. Still, it's a good survey of the subject.

(h) *The Encyclopedia of American Facts and Dates,* Gorton Carruth, Ed. (ninth edition) (HarperCollins, 1993). This is a gem of a book that I find extremely helpful. Its index makes it easy for you to find your way around.

(i) A movie and video guide. I prefer Leonard Maltin's because it's less expensive than Halliwell's and contains all the information I need. It will also be appreciated by the rest of your family, so you might have difficulty keeping it on your reference shelf.

(j) A guide to television programs, past and present. The one that was first recommended to me is *The Complete Directory to Prime Time Network Shows: 1946–Present* (fourth edition), by Tim Brooks and Earle

Marsh (Ballantine Books, 1988). The other book, which I found on my own, is called *Total Television Including Cable: A Comprehensive Guide to Programming from 1948 to the Present* (third edition), by Alex McNeil (Penguin Books, 1991). Besides being more recent than Brooks and Marsh, this volume has the virtue of including soap operas, which the other book does not.

Some Style Manuals

There are so many style manuals for so many subject areas that there is even a book that lists more than 200 of them. It is called *Style Manuals of the English-Speaking World: A Guide.* If you can't find it in your public library, you can order it from Oryx Press, Phoenix, Arizona. Here are some of my favorites:

17. *Manual of Style* (8th edition): American Medical Association (AMA), 515 North State Street, Chicago, IL 60610.

18. *Scientific Style and Format, The CBE Manual for Authors, Editors, and Publishers* (6th edition): Cambridge University Press for the Council of Biology Editors, One Illinois Center, Suite 200, 111 East Wacker Drive, Chicago, IL 60601-4298.

19. *ACS Style Guide:* American Chemical Society, 1156 16th Street NW, Washington, DC 20036.

20. *Publication Manual of the American Psychological Association* (3rd edition): American Psychological Association (APA), % Publication & Communication Office, 750 First Street NE, Washington, DC 20002.

21. *Mathematics into Type* (revised edition): American Mathematical Society, Box 6248, Providence, RI 02940. Indispensable if you're doing math or engineering editing or proofreading.

22. *Style Manual* (3rd edition): American Institute of Physics, 335 East 45th Street, New York, NY 10017.

Some of these style manuals, such as the AMA's *Manual of Style,* can be purchased in bookstores; by calling Tools of the Trade in Alexandria, Virginia, which carries a selection (see Appendix C3); or by contacting the organization in question. Prices vary, but if you're working in one of these areas, you should own the appropriate style manual.

Although we've seen what's necessary to set up your office, including the basic equipment you'll need, we haven't talked much about computers. Since computers are now as necessary to the editorial freelancer as a typewriter used to be, the subject deserves a chapter of its own. Those of you who already own a computer and the necessary software might still be interested in Chapter 4's section on a new computer editing system. The discussion of fax machines might also be of interest. After that you can proceed to Chapter 5 and start reading about clients: where to look for them, how to approach them, and other related topics. The rest of us will catch up to you shortly.

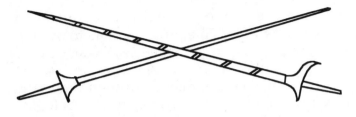

COMPUTERS AND FAXES

4

I t has taken the publishing industry a long time to make up its mind about electronic editing. One reason for this has been the difficulty of developing software that is simple to use and that gives the in-house editor sufficient control over which editorial changes are retained and which ones the authors reject. (What's to prevent authors from simply restoring their original text, leaving no trace of editorial changes?) Thus, those publishing houses that did make serious commitments to editing on disk eventually found the process too time-consuming and expensive, and so returned to editing on paper.

Even so, when I was freelancing in-house a few years ago, the rule was that if the copyeditor made more than two changes on a page, it wasn't worth the cost of correcting the author's disk, and we sent the compositor the edited manuscript instead. More recently I have found that when a publisher wants to use an author-supplied disk, the copyeditor is instructed to do a light edit; that is, to only correct spelling, punctuation, and grammatical errors, and check for consistency. In other words, follow the author's style choices rather than the house style. Still, authors are routinely asked to submit their work on a disk; in fact, book contracts almost as routinely include such a stipulation.

These days it seems as though every year I get a letter from another client saying that the company is converting to editing on disk. Many university presses have already entered the age of computer technology, and are not only editing on disk but are discussing ways in which they can collaborate in electronic publication.[1] And, many textbook publishers now make it possible for professors to put together custom-made textbooks by requesting only selected chapters; programs as wide-ranging as nationwide telephone directory searches, scientific libraries (such as the Smithsonian Institution Dinosaur Museum), and home improvement information are now on CD-ROM; and many children's books are interactive. (The term *interactive* sounds more awesome than it is, when you consider that any personal computer ever made is interactive. *Interactive* simply means that the computer or program allows the user to enter data or commands, which is accomplished either through a keyboard, a mouse, a joy stick, or a light pen.)

Therefore, whether we like it or not, as editorial freelancers we have to be computer literate as well as conversant with such other technological marvels as fax machines and modems. Computers are a very broad subject, and one that can get awfully jargony. For the purposes of this chapter, I will therefore limit myself to a basic introduction to the hardware and software that you will need to consider as an editorial freelancer. Keeping in mind the conventional wisdom that you should "buy the software you need and then buy the machine that will run it," we'll start our investigation by taking a look at software.

SOFTWARE (PROGRAMS)

There are so many different types of computer programs on the market today that it would be impossible for me to cover them all here. I will therefore limit myself to mentioning only those that are pertinent to editorial freelancing. This software falls into three categories: word processing; utilities (programs that perform specific tasks, such as retrieving deleted material and checking for viruses*); and accounting (spreadsheets and the like; these are covered in Chapter 6). In fact, the spectrum is so wide that it is possible to fill up your computer's memory with programs before you receive your first editorial assignment. It is essential, therefore, to choose only programs that are absolutely necessary.

Authors and publishers use a variety of word processing programs, most of which have the ability to convert data from one such program to another so that the data can be manipulated. For example, if you are using WordPerfect and your client sends you a book prepared in

---

*A virus is a program that, when loaded into memory, replicates itself, thus using up memory while at the same time destroying all other stored files.

Microsoft Word, this feature enables you to convert the author's disk to WordPerfect.

Some of the more popular word processing programs are:

1. *WordPerfect* for Windows or DOS. (For DOS, see below, p. 57.)
2. *Microsoft Word* for DOS.
3. *Microsoft Word* for Windows.
4. *XYWrite:* This program enjoys some currency as an editing program, but because of its high cost and the difficulty in learning it, *XYWrite* isn't used that much by publishers today, although at least one university press in New York City uses it for all of its copyediting.
5. If you're a writer, you should also consider screen capture programs (these allow you to copy what is displayed on the screen to a file or printer), such as *HiJaak Pro.*

Once you have bought a computer, you should consider subscribing to at least one computer magazine to keep yourself abreast of changes in technology. Many such publications are available, but in the beginning, especially if you're a first-time user, you might find magazines like *PC Novice* and *PC Beginner* useful. These should be supplemented by magazines that contain more advanced information, like *PC Magazine* and *PC Computing.*

Utilities

As indicated earlier, many useful ultility programs are already installed in your word processing program. They handle system-management functions such as managing disk drives, mice, program conversion, and printers. Here are some other types of utilities that are available in stores where software is sold or by mail order:

1. Housecleaning packages like *The Norton Utilities* or *PC Tools.* These packages include such functions as data recovery, compressed drive support, and maintenance and fine-tuning of system performance.
2. Antivirus programs, which make periodic checks of your system for the presence of any of the better known virus types.

3. A backup program, which automatically makes backup files of all your input data; see below for more on backing up files.

Although these functions are fairly self-explanatory, those for compressed drive support and data recovery warrant further comment. Compressed drive support is supposed to tidy up your hard disk by re-sorting files so that newer ones are stored in areas from which old ones have been deleted—that is, closer to the "center"—thereby giving you faster access to all your files. Approach these programs with caution, however, as they have been known to cause trouble—at best scrambling files; at worst ruining the hard drive—because these terms mean different things to different systems.

The purpose of the data recovery feature is easier to appreciate, since we all occasionally delete files by mistake, through carelessness or because we're in a hurry. The operative word here is *delete,* which is different from *erase.* Erasing is permanent because those data are immediately overwritten by such characters as zeros; but deleting leaves the data intact until the system, which now sees these data as expendable, overwrites them with a new file. Most word processing programs give you the ability to retrieve small blocks of data, but sometimes we want to retrieve more than that. There are therefore utility features that can restore or reconstruct "deleted" material, usually the sooner after deletion the better. This is how the high-tech spies portrayed on TV and in the movies can read deleted files on their enemies' computers. But once the space occupied by that "deleted" file has been used to store new data, the old file is beyond restoration.

Because there are so many ways that data can be lost, you should make backup copies of all your files, including the programs you're using. Although most systems make a backup file (the previous version) of everything you save, it is also a good idea to copy your files to separate disks or tapes, which you can then store in another location. Nowadays some programs automatically save every few pages of data. If your program doesn't do this and you want the convenience of not having to remember to do it yourself, you can install one of the backup programs referred to earlier.

Some reliable sources of mail-order software are PC Connection (if you're a member of a PC user group, you can save on some costs, such as shipping) and Tiger, both of which have 800 numbers, and *Computer Shopper,* a magazine that includes information on a wide range of hardware and software.

Before concluding this section, a few words about games are in order. Most of us are tempted to install them to play during a break or during our free time. Mine is called *The Magnificent Art of War at Sea.* Such games can be seductive and time-consuming, however, so I don't play mine very often. In fact, it's probably a better idea not to have games installed at all. That way you will avoid the temptation to while away precious hours on drizzly afternoons. Even a game played during a work break can easily stretch into an afternoon-long session of unproductive fun.

Choosing the software you want is only half the process. The other half consists of figuring out what hardware you will need.

HARDWARE

A survey to determine the makes of computers used by editorial freelancers would, I'm sure, reveal a wide variety of brand names: Leading Edge, IBM, Tandy, Macintosh, Epson, Hewlett-Packard, NEC, Compaq, Dell, Gateway, Northgate, to name just a few. With the exception of the Apple products, they all have a very important feature in common: they're all IBM compatible. The old distinction between Apple and IBM—buy a Mac for desktop publishing, an IBM-compatible for word processing—no longer holds true. Nowadays, WordPerfect, augmented by Windows and PageMaker, enables you to do all the desktop publishing on an IBM-compatible machine that you want.

Also, we used to be told not to buy a computer or components via mail order, because we would be unable to get a service contract or any backup help. Now one can buy machines made by Gateway and Dell, among others, over the phone. Dell will also mix and match components and will even make substitutions if you prefer one brand over another.

Although many companies provide an 800 help line, it is often difficult to get through, and once you do reach a "technician" he or she is not always as knowledgeable as you'd expect. A friend recently called one of these lines with a problem she characterized as "fairly simple," which the technician should have been able to solve without difficulty. When it became obvious that the person answering her call hadn't a clue how to help her, she managed to figure out the answer for herself. You also need to be wary of companies that are getting out of computer manufacturing or going out of business altogether.

The best advice I can give you on buying a computer is to shop around before you commit. You can start your research by reading computer magazines, such as *PC Computing* and *PC Magazine.* The former, with its "Spec Watch" feature and the practical information it provides in addition to its hardware and software reviews, can be especially helpful.

Another good source of information is friends who own computers. Ask them what equipment they own, whether they like it and why, plus what sort of service and other backup, such as free phone help, they have along with it (most dealers and software companies will answer questions about installation or other startup issues for the length of the warranty).

If you decide to go with a friend's recommendation, see if he or she will let you try out the equipment, or find a local computer store where you can noodle on a demonstration model for a while. This will give you an opportunity to see if you like the machine. While you're there, see if they'll let you try out the kinds of software you're thinking of buying. Don't be afraid to ask questions; some sales personnel can be intimidating, but don't let yourself be put off by them. One freelancer I know spent several days on the phone with a sales rep, asking questions about the various features and capabilities of the particular brand she was interested in; the rep had never heard many of those questions from other customers and had difficulty answering some of them.

When you've made up your mind what equipment will best serve your needs, don't let a salesperson talk you into buying something else.

One of the first questions to ask yourself is: What am I going to use the computer for? Will I need to access reference works? If the answer is yes, then a CD-ROM capability will be useful. Will I be mainly editing manuscripts on disk, or will I be doing desktop publishing and design? If you're going to be doing mainly editing, remember that some publishers and authors still use 5¼ inch floppy disks, so you will need to install a 5¼ inch high-density disk drive to accommodate them. You might also want to consider whether to buy a desktop computer (PC*) or a laptop.

The Desktop Computer

When I bought my desktop computer, the same consideration that leads me to rent my apartment rather than own it figured heavily in my decision: the relative ease with which I can get it serviced. If something goes wrong in my apartment, I call the superintendent; if something goes wrong with my computer, I just carry it over to the nearest Radio Shack store, and they fix it. But ease or accessibility of service, while

---

* Here PC means "personal computer," not the IBM PC, where the initials also stand for personal computer.

important, is not the only feature you should look for. Here is a run-down of some additional ones you'll want to keep in mind when choosing your desktop computer:

Capacity. Buy the most memory and the largest hard drive you can afford. (Memory, or RAM [random access memory], or main memory, refers to a computer's storage capacity and/or the chips that hold the data; hard drive, or hard disk drive, or Winchester [the name of the hard drive technology developed in 1973 by IBM] drive, is the comput-er's permanent memory.)

DOS (Version 6.2 or later). DOS, or disk operating system, is the oper-ating system used by IBM-compatible PCs. It can also be called MS-DOS (the standard operating system developed by Microsoft [MS] for use on IBM-compatible PCs) or PC-DOS (an almost identical system sold by IBM).

A color monitor. The component that looks like a TV screen on which you see your input.

A VGA (video graphics array) adapter. The VGA, which comes installed on most computers these days, is a display system for use on IBM PCs and clones. It provides better resolution on both text and graphics modes, and a greater color palette, than earlier systems.

A mini tower or desktop unit. These contain the disk drives, as well as the slots and bays necessary for further expansion. If you decide to buy a mini tower, look for front-panel access.

Hard disk and tape backup. Called "hard" so it won't be confused with the "soft" or floppy disk, it is a magnetic disk that comes installed in computers. It is used to store data, just like a floppy, only its memory capacity is greater (it can store up to 3000 megabytes [MB] as opposed to the floppy's maximum of 20MB) and it's faster than a floppy.

A 3½ inch high-density disk drive. (As indicated earlier, you may also want to have a 5¼ inch high-density drive installed.)

Documentation, disks, and registration cards for any installed software.

Cables. These are used to attach the various components to each other and to the source of electricity. They should be provided as part of the package when you're buying the computer. If you don't make sure of this at the time of purchase, you may have to pay for one or more of them later.

A power-strip surge protector to protect the power supply against elec-trical surges that can cause loss of all the data you've input but not yet saved.

Built-in ports (serial, parallel, mouse). A port is the place on a computer (also called an interface) where you attach a peripheral device, such as a mouse or a printer.

A printer. A laser printer gives the best-quality output; but these days ink jet and dot-matrix printers also produce letter-quality and near-letter-quality output, respectively). If you opt for a dot-matrix-type printer, be sure it is at least 24 pin, which produces the best quality print.

A mouse and mousepad. The mouse is a small attachment that is used, instead of the keyboard, to give instructions to the computer. By rolling it along the desktop, you move the pointer (a small arrow) to position it at a desired location. It is called a mouse because its shape is reminiscent of a mouse, and the cord attaching it to the computer suggests a mouse's tail. The mousepad is a square-shaped piece of rubberized material (about 7¼" by 7½") on which the mouse sits. It offers better traction for the mouse than some surfaces, such as wood or glass, and therefore the mouse can be manipulated with greater precision.

Two others warrant serious consideration:

A modem, either internal or external. This device enables you to transmit data over a standard telephone line. Modems are essential if you want to be on the Internet or subscribe to a bulletin board or if you want to directly upload or download information to or from another computer. If you want to attach a modem to your computer, your machine will need to be equipped with an RS-232 port, but since most PCs have them, this shouldn't be a problem. A baud rate (the speed with which the modem can send and receive data) of 9600 bps (bits per second) should be sufficient. On the other hand, if you want to use the fax feature on your computer, you will need to get a fax modem that can double as a regular modem (for more on fax modems, see the last section of this chapter).

CD-ROM (compact disc read-only memory). I mention this only because, though it is not always necessary, some editorial freelancers are acquiring CD-ROM players in anticipation of future need. A CD-ROM is an optical disk that can store large amounts of data, up to 250,000 text pages. Once recorded (you need a special machine to accomplish this), the data cannot be erased, although erasable optical disk technology is currently being developed. Because of its large storage capacity, CD-ROM was first used for recording multivolume encyclopedias, including their graphics. Another advantage is that, because of uniform size and format, it is possible for any CD to be played on virtually any CD-ROM player. I'm not recommending that you rush out and buy a CD-ROM player, but you should be aware that in many circles erasable CDs are considered the storage device of the future.

The Laptop Computer

Although when we think of computers we generally mean the desktop type, nowadays many people are using laptops as their only computer. Laptops are less expensive than desktops, take up less space, are portable (so you can use them at a client's office or on a train), and can plug into a monitor. Their main drawback is that they tend to be powered by a battery, making battery life a major consideration, especially because when the battery dies all unsaved data are lost.

If you're considering getting a laptop, research it just as you would a desktop. As an additional aid, here are some things to think about and look for:

Notebook versus subnotebook. If you're going to use it as your only computer, buy a notebook rather than a subnotebook, and be sure you can plug it into a monitor. Notebooks weigh less than 9 pounds and have at least 9½ inch screens; subnotebooks weigh 4 pounds or less and have 7½ inch screens.

Color versus monochrome screen.

Battery life. These computers come with battery packs; the batteries need to be recharged every few hours, so ask the dealer how many hours the computer can safely operate between recharges.

Display type. Here you're looking for a 9½ inch or larger back-lit, dual-scan, passive- or active-matrix color LCD (liquid crystal display) with accelerated local bus video (a structure that speeds up the system's performance); also look for adjustable contrast and brightness controls.

Be sure the screen is really clear. I say this because you will find that some screens have too much glare (many people find monochrome screens easier on their eyes than color screens; others claim that once they find the right combination of hues [e.g., gray letters on a blue background], color is more restful). In addition, letters sometimes aren't as sharp as they might be.

Keyboard size. Keyboard sizes vary according to the size of the machine, but on most notebooks they are the approximate width of the main pad on a desktop keyboard. Although the major letter and number keys are about normal size, some other keys, such as the cursor (arrow) and function keys, are about half normal size. Since some people complain that their fingers "fall off" these smaller keys, you should make sure this won't be a problem for you. Also in the interests of saving space, most of these computers have an FN key—this is not a function (F) key—that has to be pressed along with another key in order to accomplish certain routine functions.

Amount of memory. This is a judgment call based on what you're planning to use the computer for, but remember it's better to have too much than too little memory. Notebooks come with 8 megabytes (MB) of memory, expandable to 20MB; subnotebooks come with 4MB, expandable to 16MB.

Size of the hard disk. You want at least 120MB.

Check to be sure the computer can be connected to a printer. If it can, ask about cables.

The discussion in this and the previous section should be sufficient to get you started with computers and set you up with the types of equipment you will need to be computer-ready for your clients.

WAY OF THE FUTURE?

I have heard it said that most editing programs are basically redlining programs and that, as one editorial freelancer puts it, "They're for lawyers, not editors."

Simply put, redlining means marking edited text so that the in-house editor and the author can see which is original text and which has been worked on. In other words, redlining is to computers as the highlighting pen is to paper. The redlined text often appears on your screen in a special color or in boldface. In my word processing program the redlined text is lightly covered by x's or some other symbol of my choosing. A large number of word processors have an automatic redlining feature that allows the word processor to compare two documents and then redline any differences. Whatever the case, when you edit on a disk, you'll have to know how to redline altered text.

The editorial functions of word processing programs that once prompted remarks like the one quoted above may no longer be as limited as they were, however. For example, Microsoft Word's Revise/Annotate features allow you to, among other things, put comments in a book as annotations, automatically mark and keep separate track of revisions by several people, print the book with or without revisions showing, and review and accept or reject each revision or all of them.

Responding to the need for a dedicated editing program that works well, the folks at Advanced Pen Technologies (APT; founded in 1991) developed a system specifically for copyediting. After consulting with editors and other publishing personnel, they came up with a system that, in the words of a 1993 article in *The Seybold Report on Desktop Publishing*, "could change the way editing of books and journals is done."[2] First there is the hardware, an IBM ThinkPad 710T pen computer (basically a notebook-size laptop) plus such peripherals as a keyboard, a wire rack to rest the computer on when it's not in use, and a case. This equipment is both lightweight and sturdy—it can withstand the shock of being dropped or knocked to the floor.

But the genius of this system lies in the software. PenEdit can read any software an author is likely to use, and then some, and at the conclusion of editing it can code the document by any system a printer is likely to use. The real beauty of PenEdit, however, is that it allows you to edit with a light pen, using familiar copyediting marks. For example, if you want to delete a character, you use the light pen to draw a pigtail on that character just as you would with your pencil on a manuscript page. To boldface, draw a "B" on the word or text you want to highlight; to italicize, draw an "I." A "U" underlines, an "N" restores normal typeface, and an "E" (for stet) undoes a change. You can add text by writing it in a separate file called a notepad; the system then inserts the new text where you want it in the body of the manuscript. These additions appear in a font that looks like handwritten text.

Because you use handwritten characters as commands, etc., the system can be "trained" to distinguish among individual printing styles. Thus, when I tried out the system during a hands-on session, the machine had some difficulty reading my printing because it had been trained by one of the company's vice presidents to read *his* printing. Some other editing features include the ability to make global changes, insert design codes, and make author queries (which it marks in the manuscript with an icon and prints as a separate document). It also includes a spell checker and thesaurus. And, as of this writing, APT is planning to bring out a Windows version in the summer of 1995, with free upgrades for current owners.

As you might expect, the PenEdit system is at present quite expensive; the list price of $6500 includes hardware, software, training, service, and free upgrades for a year. Although you could buy PenEdit on a lease-purchase plan that APT makes available, at this point in the development of this technology it would be best to proceed with caution. Another option suggested by APT is for the publisher to purchase the equipment and loan it out to freelancers. APT would then supply training for any freelancers sent by a company that has purchased PenEdit. All this may be moot, however, since APT has announced that the next edition (update) will be a stand-alone package that will operate only on Windows-capable computers.

The question remains as to whether the system benefits the editorial freelancer, who will be providing a service in less time than before but at the same pay. Many freelancers may balk at such a situation. One suggestion is higher fees to cover the costs of lost time as well as for a skill that is not shared by all freelancers.

Meanwhile, PenEdit has been taken up by several publishing houses, including Viking (which has used it to copyedit at least one novel), Warner Books, Penguin, Facts on File, and Stoddart (Canada). Some other publishing houses are interested but are as yet uncommitted.

It will be interesting to see if PenEdit does indeed represent the way of the future, or if it is just another anomaly along the way—but one that may have had a role in prompting the major software producers to make their products more editor-friendly.

THE FAX

Most freelance writers I know, and a growing number of the editors, find the fax machine an indispensable tool. My major problem with faxes is that the paper on which most transmissions are received is the "rubberized" thermal type, which is impossible to work on, making it necessary to photocopy the entire document before use. Also the print quality is sometimes so poor that the document is difficult or impossible to read, and art sent by fax is not camera-ready. Fax transmissions also have to be stored carefully, as prolonged exposure to light will cause the print to fade—another reason why they should be copied upon receipt. Of course there are plain-paper faxes, but these tend to be too expensive for most freelancers.

When choosing your fax machine you need to answer the following questions:

- Do I want a fax machine or a fax modem?
- Do I want a dedicated fax or one with an answering machine attached?
- Do I want one with a phone or just a jack to plug in my own phone?
- Do I want one that operates on my existing phone line, or do I want a separate line for it? (See Chapter 3 for more on this question.)
- Do I want a plain-paper or thermal fax?
- What does the built-in copier do?
- Does the model I like have the ability to differentiate between fax transmissions and regular phone calls, or do I need to buy a separate converter?

Here is a short list of some other things to consider when buying a fax:

The manufacturer's reputation.
The service arrangements available.

The machine's memory capacity. There are two main areas where faxes use memory. The first is for remembering telephone numbers for automatic dialing; that is, how many numbers will it store? The other applies only to plain-paper faxes, and concerns the number of pages (expressed as, for example, "twenty-page memory") the machine can store should it run out of paper or ink while receiving. This is particularly critical when you are being sent a twenty- or thirty-page document while you're out or in the wee hours after midnight and the machine runs out of paper after receiving only six pages.

The print resolution: 203 by 98 dpi (dots per inch) or 203 by 196 dpi.

Speed: 4800 bps (bits per second) or 9600 bps.

Printer type: The less expensive thermal type, or the costlier plain-paper type.

Paper size: Letter or legal size, 8.5 inches wide or 10.1 inches wide; some machines take only the 8.5 inch size.

Paper cutter: This is necessary because most thermal paper comes in rolls. Even so, portable faxes and some less expensive faxes are not equipped with a cutter.

Paper feeder: This is necessary if you're going to be making multiple-page transmissions and don't want to have to feed each page into the machine by hand.

Autodialing: This feature is handy if you want to preset the machine to transmit late at night when phone rates are lower.

The number of sheets the paper tray will hold (for plain-paper faxes).

Earlier in this section we referred to the fax modem, but did not define it. Although some computers come with fax modems (fax boards) installed, they can also be attached externally. These devices allow you to transmit electronic data just like other faxes, but they differ from regular modems in that they are designed to transmit to fax machines or to another fax modem, rather than to a computer. Although fax modems are less expensive than regular fax machines, always send at 9600 bps, are more convenient if your documents are already in electronic form, and produce superior image quality, you cannot use them to transmit paper documents unless you also have a separate optical scanner. The cost of such a scanner, however, negates the fax modem's price advantage. Also received documents require large amounts of memory—approximately 100 kilobytes (K) per page.

Now that we've investigated many of the more practical areas of editorial freelancing, it's time to consider the business aspects. We begin this investigation in the next chapter, which deals with ways of finding and keeping clients.

NOTES

1. John F. Baker, "UPs View Issues of Survival in Electronic Age," *Publishers Weekly,* July 11, 1994, p. 16.
2. George A. Alexander, "Applied Technology: A Closer Look at PenEdit," *The Seybold Report on Desktop Publishing,* vol. 8, no. 3, November 8, 1993, 8 pp.

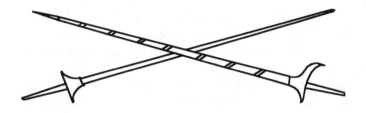

FINDING AND KEEPING CLIENTS 5

For the new freelancer, finding clients is much like getting charge accounts back in the days before the credit explosion. You needed to have one in order to get one. If you could show Lord & Taylor that you were a good credit risk, however, they weren't as finicky as other department stores. And once you had an account there, it was fairly easy to get one at Macy's or Bloomingdale's, too.

To continue the analogy, you might say that for the New York area McGraw-Hill was the Lord & Taylor of the text and professional book publishers. By this I mean that in 1976 McGraw still trained inexperienced freelancers, provided that they had passed the copy-editing test. And once you had McGraw-Hill as a client, your chances of expanding your client list were almost 100 percent. But even with that avenue available to the beginning editorial freelancer, it was not easy to find clients—and things haven't changed much in that regard.

Not surprisingly, one of the questions newcomers ask most often is "Where—and how—do I find clients?" There are no hard-and-fast answers to this question, but this chapter contains some pointers that should prove helpful.

FINDING CLIENTS

Looked at in one way, every person, company, or nonprofit organization is a potential client—from the graduate student who needs to have a dissertation proofread to a company that needs someone to write its annual report.

One caveat regarding individuals as clients (students, unpublished novelists, grant seekers, etc.): exercise caution and be prepared for the worst. I realize that some people are making a good living editing book manuscripts before they go to agents or publishers, but there is another side to this situation that you should be aware of. When I was managing the EFA Job Phone Service we had listings from, among others, the daughter of the other Great Imposter ("not Ferdinand Demara, whom Tony Curtis played in the movies"*), Liberace's cousin (after Liberace died), and the now-grown-up Lindbergh baby, all wanting someone to write their stories. Like others of their ilk, they expected the writer to work "on spec"†—in this case, a percentage of future royalties. Needless to say, they had few takers, since most professional writers want to be paid an hourly or project rate (see Chapter 7) while they are doing the job.

Sometimes individuals seeking freelance help find a rate of, say, $20 an hour too steep for their budgets. Or they might hire you and then, after seeing a chapter or two and your bill, try and find some way (usually disagreeable) of defaulting on payment. For example, they could claim that money was never talked about, because if it had been, they never would have agreed to the amount you charged them, or they might say they were unhappy with the way you did the job and flatly refuse to pay you for it. One extreme case was the woman who hired a man to ghostwrite a book about her experiences as a patient in a hospital. He drafted a chapter and charged her $20 for his time, which she paid. She then decided she didn't like his work and started making threatening phone calls demanding that he return her money. She told him that she was from Haiti and that her friends practiced voodoo. At one point he received a dead animal on a card in the mail—a voodoo sign that she was after him—and his apartment was broken into several times. Finally, to stop the madness, the company that had put them together to begin with sent her the $20 and the incidents stopped.

---

* Both Demara and this lister's father had spent their lives successfully practicing professions—penology, surgery, and the like—for which they had no formal training, always gaining the respect of their "colleagues."

† "On spec" means to work on speculation, that is, the promise of a percentage of future profits, such as an advance or royalties.

Besides individuals, there are three other major types of clients: people you know, publishing houses of various descriptions (trade, textbook, university presses, etc.), and corporations. Filling the gaps between these three types are myriad other sources—small print shops, hospitals, nonprofit organizations, stock brokerage houses, law firms, direct mail companies, advertising agencies, banks, to name a few—but, since the same techniques are used for approaching all of these, for the purposes of this book we'll stay with the larger groups.

People You Know

The most obvious network to tap is people you know. If you're starting fresh and have no professional editorial experience, then you probably won't have any personal contacts—but your friends or family might, especially if you live in New York, Boston, San Francisco, or other large centers of publishing. For example, when I started looking for a job in publishing, I discovered that my half-sister's stepdaughter worked for Stein & Day. Even though I had a close personal relationship with my sister, and had seen her at least once a week for the previous three years, I had never known about this contact before. In another case a colleague told me of the time in 1972 when she worked for Dean Witter. Her boss's secretary knew someone who worked at Appleton. When my friend went freelance, she called the Appleton editor, who gave her the names of managing editors at five textbook publishers, all of whom gave her copyediting tests.

The returns may not always be this great, but as I said at the beginning of the chapter, once you have one client, it's easier to get more clients. My career has been advanced more by referrals than by my approaching possible new employers, but most freelancers—even those with many years of experience and numerous clients—make it a practice to keep sending out letters and making phone calls in order to expand their client lists.

Corporations

The most difficult hurdle to be overcome when you're seeking assignments from large companies is the most basic one— finding the specific person (and his or her title) you should approach. Another is being told to go through the Personnel Department. In the first case, the Director of Publications, although bearing a promising title, may head a department whose staff does all the editorial work; also, Publications or Communications Departments are often so busy they don't have time to stop and figure out where they can use a freelancer, even though they may need or could use one. On the other hand, a junior vice president somewhere may have been tapped to handle the company newsletter and several brochures single-handed because he once served as editor of his college literary magazine. This person would welcome some help, if he only knew where to find it. In other words, the company publications that need your services are likely being handled by people you wouldn't find by merely perusing a list of corporate officers and department heads.

Very often a switchboard operator or receptionist can steer you in the right direction, though this process may require patience, diplomacy, persistence, and definitely a clear and concise statement of what it is you're looking for. Although the people on the switchboard have a better feel for who does what than do workers in specific departments, they don't have time to listen to long-winded explanations. But whatever happens, don't allow yourself to be shunted into the Personnel Department; that's the kiss of death. You'll never hear from them, because they don't know where to send you, and pretty soon they won't even remember you. None of this is their fault; besides the fact that freelancers and other independent contractors fall into a category that personnel workers are not trained to deal with, these people usually aren't given sufficient detail about the jobs they're trying to fill. For example, when asked to hire an editor, they might be told to look for someone who is detail-oriented and can do the job in the least amount of time. They will therefore invariably pass over the best qualified applicant for one who may have no real editorial experience but who meets the two basic criteria.

One advantage you have over someone looking for work in book publishing is that personnel in corporations don't have the same high-level of turnover as do editors in the more traditional areas of publishing. Therefore, once you've found the right person, chances are not only that that individual will still be in place, but that you'll be working with him or her for almost as long as you work for that company.

Also, remember what we said in Chapter 2 about corporations not making the same distinctions between editor, copyeditor, and proofreader as do publishers. To them an editor is someone who can do everything from copyediting to proofreading to editing to substantive editing. Therefore, if you are a substantive editor, present yourself as a writer, while if you're only comfortable doing the chores usually expected of copyeditors (which to a corporate client is practically the same as a proofreader), make it clear that you don't do writing and heavy editing. Once they understand what it is you do, however, and they like your work, you can develop a long-term working relationship.

Once you've identified the person you need to contact, proceed as discussed later in this chapter. That is, send your résumé with a cover letter, then, a few days later, follow up with a phone call. Insist on talking to the person you want to see. Be persistent, but not pushy. Your goal is to get an interview. After the interview, send a thank-you letter. If you don't hear anything within a reasonable time, check in with another phone call. If the people you contact use freelancers, it never hurts to keep your name fresh in their minds.

Publishers

In publishing it's somewhat easier to identify the correct person to approach for freelance work than it is in the corporate world. You can either look the company up in *Literary Market Place* (LMP) to find the name of the Managing Editor or the Copy Chief, or you can call the company and ask for the name and title of the person to whom you should send your query. The latter method is more certain, because even the latest edition of LMP is apt to be out of date, since editors move around so frequently.

Of course there are other places besides LMP where you can look for editorial work. One of my friends reads the want ads in the *New York Times* every Sunday, just to see what's available. When reading these ads, you do need to be aware that the listers are not always clear about exactly what it is they're looking for. Many ads start with the all-caps lead, EDITOR, but a close reading soon reveals that what they really want is a writer. Although most ads are legitimate, some are plants designed to get you into an employment agency. At best it's a frustrating process, however. When I was first looking for a job, I'd sometimes be the first one at the agency on the day after seeing a promising ad, only to be told that the job I wanted was no longer available.

Editorial jobs are listed under three main categories: editor, proofreader, and writer, but you should also scan public relations, advertising, legal (for legal proofreading), and any other areas where you think publishing-related jobs might be listed. But you can't rely solely, or even mainly, on these ads—the process is much too frustrating and unreliable.

The library is a good place to seek out other sources. For instance, although you can't buy it on the newsstand, *Publishers Weekly* (PW), which, along with *Adweek*, is a good place both to find ads and to list your availability, can be found in the library (see the final section of this chapter for more ideas on where you can list). And while you're there, ask to see other publications that might contain useful information on specific areas. For example, there are directories and indexes for practically everything, including *Reader's Guide to Periodical Literature* (an index of general interest magazines listed alphabetically by subject area, such as Education), *The International Encyclopedia of Company Histories*, *The Directory of Associations*, *Job Outlook*, and my personal favorite, *Job Hunter's Sourcebook*, which, under Writers and Editors, includes such headings as Sources of Help-Wanted Ads; Placement Referral Sources; Employer Directories and Networking Lists; Handbooks and Manuals; Employment Agencies and Search Firms; Other Leads. See Appendix C1 for other such sources. The library is probably the last place you'd think to look for sources of work, but it should be one of the first places you visit. If used properly, it can be a treasure house. Just tell the librarian what you're looking for—that's what they're there for, and they will often go out of their way to help you find what you need.

Another source to consider is the job banks run by professional associations, such as Washington Independent Writers, American Society of Journalists and Authors (Dial-a-Writer), Chicago Women in Publishing (Jobvine), and Editorial Freelancers Association (Job Phone). At least in the case of EFA, you need to be a member of the association and a subscriber in order to receive information about the jobs, though anybody can listen to the listings. And all of them charge something to use their services, but whatever the cost, it's worth it to have access to the jobs listed.

Before moving on to ways of approaching new sources of work, there is one more method of finding clients that should be mentioned. I have heard of at least one editorial freelancer who occasionally uses electronic bulletin boards (BBSs) and the Internet to get work. It should be emphasized, however, that this is not accomplished through any sort of advertising, which is against electronic etiquette and would result in the offender being severely "flamed" (criticized), but develops from contacts made through electronic networking.

In the case I'm thinking of, the jobs come after an electronic relationship has been established on the basis of conversation in a public forum, during which time the freelancer discovers whether the other person is literate and articulate. Thus, if it comes up later that the other person has some writing that needs looking at, the freelancer contacts her correspondent via private E-mail in which she suggests that the other send the piece "electronically or via 'snail mail'." After looking at the writing to see if she feels she can make a contribution, the freelancer uses the BBS to send a short evaluation, for which there's no charge. After that, all things being agreeable, they proceed to a discussion of terms, which include the freelancer's regular rate. "This approach has worked very well because it's so low pressure on both sides, and because it's initiated on the basis of a previously established electronic acquaintance."

THE APPROACH

All well and good, you may be saying, but what steps do I need to take? Should I call or write? If both, in what order? What should I say? And how in the world do you write a résumé anyway?

The answer to this last question is that there is no one right way. Styles can range from the traditional chronological listing of education and employment history to the letter résumé to some very creative ones, often produced with the help of computers. My only caveat on the latter is not to get too creative with typefaces, typesizes, and icons.

However, it is not my purpose here to give a crash course in résumé writing—there are enough of these already, viz., among myriad others, *Who's Hiring Who? How to Find that Job Fast,* by Richard Lathrop (Ten Speed Press, most recent edition) and the more familiar *What Color Is Your Parachute?*, by Richard Nelson Bolles (Ten Speed Press, latest edition by year). Instead, I offer the following list of some of the things that should be included in a résumé:

- Your name, address, phone and fax (if appropriate) numbers
- Name(s) of former employer(s)
- Name(s) of clients, past and present
- Your editorial skills or, if you're new to the field, other skills (such as secretarial) that will make you attractive to a prospective employer
- Your computer literacy; that is, what kind of computer you own (if any) and the name(s) of the program(s) you own or can operate
- Any special-interest areas in which you are knowledgeable, such as movies of the 1920s and 1930s
- Titles of books or articles you've published, as well as where or by whom and date of publication
- A line saying "References upon request."

And some optional items:

- Dates of employment
- College(s) attended and date(s) of graduation
- Degree(s) earned

- The names, titles, name of company where employed,
  and phone numbers of your references; that is, three
  people (not relatives) who are willing to speak for
  you or write letters of recommendation upon request.

Now that you've targeted potential sources of work, let's move on to answer the question of how to make the approach. The best way to proceed is to do a saturation mailing. In other words, send your résumé, with your business card attached, to everyone on your list. Include a cover letter, in which you state your interest in working for that company and close by saying you'll call in a few days to be sure your query was received. Your object in all this is to get an interview, so when you make your call, be polite but persistent.

As a warning about the way you word your opus, one of my colleagues tells a story about a letter the publisher she worked for received from a potential freelancer. The writer said that the company's surprisingly low standard of editing had ruined her favorite author's most recent book. She enclosed a two-page analysis of the kinds of errors she meant, most of which on close examination proved not to be errors after all, but rather her misinterpretations of the relevant rules of grammar. Needless to say, her offer that she be hired as a copyeditor was not accepted.

The idea itself is a valid ploy, but the letter needs to be worded diplomatically so as not to be patronizing or insulting—and it has to be carefully proofread. Letters and résumés containing typos and grammatical errors do not create a good first impression. Remember, the goal is to court, not alienate, the client.

INTERVIEWING

Although perhaps used less often than it once was, the interview can still be an important step in finding new clients because it is here that you get a chance both to sell yourself and to assess the client. In fact, on most occasions when I get assignments from new clients, they request that I come in to pick up the work so they can get a look at me. Personal contact is very important in the client-freelancer relationship, especially in the early stages.

I think the two factors that have clinched jobs for me during interviews are being relaxed (if only in appearance) and projecting confidence. For example, I was once called about a proofreading job on an intermediate algebra book. When I arrived at the editor's office, he asked me if I could handle a job with a lot of math in it. I said I could. He then handed me some galley pages and asked if I foresaw any difficulty in dealing with the material. I looked through them and said no. After all, there was nothing there I hadn't encountered before. He told me later that what sold him on me was that when he confronted me with the actual math, I didn't blanch. It seems he'd been stung at least once by someone who told him he or she could do the job, but turned out to have little experience with math. The editor had therefore begun showing interviewees galleys to test their veracity.

This story brings up a touchy subject—shading the truth on the résumé and during interviews. Of course everybody exaggerates their abilities somewhat in order to get the job. If your assurances aren't too overstated, you can usually muddle through and learn something along the way. But this practice can backfire, as we'll see at the beginning of Chapter 6, in which case you not only hurt the client but also damage your own reputation. I would therefore recommend that you stay as close to the truth as possible.

Prepare Yourself

It's always a good idea to do some preparation before going to an interview. When I had my very first one, I had no idea what to expect or what would be expected of me. I'd walked into Macmillan on the chance they might have an opening, only to find they were interviewing that day for a production editor (see Chapter 1). I agreed to be interviewed, but was hesitant and unsure of myself. For example, when he asked about job experience, I didn't know how to respond because after graduation from college, and except for two years' active service in the Navy, I had spent the previous eight years trying to make it as a fiction writer. He tried to give me examples of what he was looking for, but I was feeling defensive about not having an employment record, and therefore couldn't speak with assurance about the experience I did have. He must have seen something in me, however, because he didn't stop the interview, but continued much like a teacher giving a slow student clues to the correct answers without stating them outright. Obviously I didn't get the job, but I did get some valuable information on what would be expected of me in the future. (As an aside, I had lunch with my brother afterward, and he advised me not to let the experience discourage me from trying again. I say the same to you. Job hunting can be frustrating and hard on one's self-esteem, but don't let these considerations stop you. Try and learn from your "failures" so you'll be better prepared for the next time.)

One way to prepare is to rehearse your answers to questions you think you might be asked. Review your skills and qualifications. Also make sure you have certain basic information, even if it may not be necessary for getting freelance work. I used to carry with me a three-by-five-inch index card on which I'd recorded important dates (e.g., my parents' birth and death dates), my Social Security number, and other information necessary for filling out forms.

When you're packing your briefcase in preparation for the interview, remember to include a copy of your résumé; a separate list of books, magazines, journals, or projects you've worked on, if any; and writing and/or editing samples. Writing samples may consist of legible photocopies of articles or stories you've had published; as samples of your editing, you could take photocopies of manuscript pages you've edited. Obviously, if you're just beginning, you're not going to have samples. I've never supplied editing samples, and have never felt that the lack was the cause of my not getting a particular job.

One of the panelists at an EFA meeting once suggested that "if you have the time prior to an interview, check out the neighborhood, the office, the lobby, and how people answer the phone."[1] Doing so can give you valuable insights into whether you'd be comfortable working for the company, especially if you would be required to spend large amounts of time there or in the area.

A Word on Attire and Language

One of the perks of being a freelancer is being able to work in casual clothes. My first couple of hours at my desk each day are spent in my bathrobe. You can also work all day without shaving or even bathing, if you want. But when you're going to a client's office, whether for an interview or just to pick up a project, you should dress in a businesslike fashion and be well groomed (but don't overdo the perfume or aftershave). While styles of dress may vary according to the company's location, a good general rule for men is that "businesslike" means a suit or jacket and tie and shined shoes. Since not all women feel comfortable wearing tailored business suits, their choice of outfit is a bit more flexible, but should be aimed at achieving the same effect.

I have been told that I always looked well dressed, until you saw my shoes. I notice the same thing in both men and women, who are well dressed from the ankles up. But ill-considered footwear is only one of many points of appearance that can kill a professional impression; some others are messy hair, ugly clothes, and (to me, at least) the recently fashionable two-day growth of beard.

Being in the business we're in, we're all well aware that standards of verbal and written communication have slipped considerably, often aided by insufficient attention paid to grammar and composition in secondary schools, the popular press, including magazines, and, especially, the broadcast media. Be that as it may, one of the prime functions of editors is to maintain the highest standards of the language. Therefore, when you go for an interview, do not talk like a teenager. By this I mean don't use such locutions as "Then he goes 'blah-blah,' so I went 'blah-blah'" or "This job is like just perfect for me"—you get the picture.

The Subject of Money

The always-difficult-to-deal-with subject of money is bound to come up during the interview, so be prepared to cite your hourly or project rate. (See Chapter 7 for information on determining your rate.) Often, however, the client will tell you what rate they're prepared to pay. If the rate you want is higher, say so, but don't make it sound final. You want to leave yourself room to negotiate if the client balks at your price. If you think you can accept a negotiated compromise without being grumpy about underselling yourself, then accept the offer. If not, I suggest that you say no. Freelancing is hard enough without putting the extra strain of suppressed anger on your heart and stomach lining. In fact, if more freelancers said no to unacceptable rates, the general level of rates might rise.

Of course it sometimes happens that the end of the interview is approaching and money hasn't been mentioned yet. Remember that the interviewer is probably as nervous about discussing money as you are, and is trying to avoid the subject—or has simply forgotten it. To avoid misunderstandings, it is best to reach an agreement at this stage, even if you have to raise the subject yourself. In such situations, I usually say something like, "We haven't said anything about money" or "I think I should mention that my rate is thus and so." Such statements may not be particularly elegant, but at least the subject is on the table and you can proceed from there.

Tests

You should be prepared to take a copyediting/proofreading test (see Appendix A), if that's the kind of work you're applying for. Until I worked two days a week as an assistant to the Managing Editor at Van Nostrand Reinhold (VNR), I had always considered these tests to be a waste of time because, like many seasoned freelancers, I felt I was too experienced to be asked to take them. Once I was in the position of correcting them and evaluating the results, however, I discovered that they are a good indicator of an applicant's potential. I was also surprised to find that I could often make this determination more accurately from the test than from the résumé.

Here are two other opinions, one from a freelancer, the other from a then recently retired Senior Editor at *Newsweek*. Both quotes are taken from the "Opinions" column in the May/June 1981 issue of the *EFA Newsletter:*[2]

> "They were helpful to me when I was entering freelancing; I found out what was expected. I object to the great length of some tests, and think they're humiliating for someone with references and experience." (Carol Barko)

> "I've given tests and found them valuable, though arbitrary and artificial. For example, they don't test speed directly. Tests should be used along with other factors, such as interviews. They do show knowledge of grammar and usage, and some factual knowledge (for example, about New York City). They're not good in evaluating knowledge of style, because each house has a different style. A freelancer shouldn't object to tests if he or she is trying to move into a different area, such as magazines." (Albert McCollough)

These tests are time-consuming, but I've rarely heard of freelancers being paid for the hours spent on them. Like the interview, they are considered part of the cost of getting a job. Therefore, when asked to take one, don't treat it too casually. I once took both the copyediting and proofreading tests for the college division at a large publishing house. I fear I did a cursory job, thinking my experience would see me through. Needless to say, I failed both tests miserably, and my reward was no job and a large helping of humble pie.

As an alternative to the copyediting test, some publishers will ask you to copyedit perhaps two chapters (or between fifty and one hundred pages) of the manuscript for evaluation before hiring you. If you're successful, you just add the time spent to your bill; if you're not, they will generally pay you for your time anyway. For example, a few years ago, I and some other technical editors I know were approached by an engineering society about "auditioning" for a job rewriting a professional-level engineering book. They sent us about ten pages and asked us to submit a bill with the finished work. I talked to one or two of the others afterwards, but I never heard who got the job. Before getting involved in this kind of arrangement, however, be sure that you are going to be paid. I've heard of situations where freelancers who have been asked to edit a few pages of a short manuscript without pay as a test—and who were not hired—have had reason to suspect that the client was attempting to get the work edited for free by giving small batches of pages to several different applicants.

Follow-up

The last step is to write a short letter thanking the interviewer for taking the time to see you. In it, you can recall some of the highlights of the interview, just to spotlight your qualifications. The thank-you letter is good manners and creates a favorable impression in the mind of the interviewer. It could even be the straw that tips the scale in your favor.

If you don't hear anything within a reasonable period, and you want to work for that particular client (and don't think you shot yourself in the foot during the interview), call and ask if they have made their decision. Sometimes, even if that job has been assigned, there is another one in the pipeline. At the very least, you'll have reminded them of your existence, which is never a bad idea in this business.

A final reminder: Consider each interview a rehearsal for the next one. In fact, some people I know think it's a good idea to go to interviews even when they've got enough work, just to maintain the skill.

MARKETING YOURSELF

Once you've acquired a couple of steady clients, and even if they're keeping you constantly busy, don't stop marketing yourself. One of the worst mistakes freelancers make is to become complacent, assuming that their current clients will keep them busy forever. This simply does not happen. For example, one of the first freelancers I met worked exclusively for one publishing house because the Copy Chief was his friend. After she died, however, he had to start the process of finding clients all over again—from scratch. Another well-established editor left on vacation one year secure in the knowledge that she had two steady, high-paying clients— Harper & Row and Deloitte Haskins & Sells. When she returned two weeks later, *both* of them had undergone mergers, and the work flow dried up.

The Telephone and Other Simple Aids

The first and most obvious way to market yourself is to make a brief phone call from time to time to remind your current clients that you're still available. Sometimes these calls produce work immediately. The first client I contacted after my in-house job at VNR ended had two jobs coming along, both of which she offered me as soon as I told her I was "back in the freelance pool."

Sending a greeting card during the holiday season also creates a good impression, as would a congratulatory card or phone call on a promotion or a birthday. Or arrange to occasionally take your contacts to lunch.

Earlier I mentioned a friend who reads the want ads every Sunday even though she freelances full-time for one client. She also checks to see what jobs are available on the EFA Job Phone. (Since you need to be an EFA member and a Job Phone subscriber in order to get contact information for these jobs, I only mention it as a possible resource.) And from time to time she either answers some of the newspaper ads or sends letters to potential clients she finds in various directories in the library.

Every freelancer, no matter what his or her situation, would benefit from this latter practice. You should never stop looking for new sources of work, and sending out query letters on a regular basis is an excellent way to do it. It also keeps your name active in the publishing universe.

Networking

Another form of continuous marketing of oneself is networking, which can be defined as contacting someone by letter or phone, or talking to another person in a social situation about what you do. In other words, networking is keeping in touch with clients and other freelancers. As you know, many freelance jobs are acquired by word of mouth. An editor makes a call when he or she needs a freelancer for a certain job, but if that freelancer is too busy to take it on, the caller will often ask for a recommendation. Or you might be chatting with a freelancer who remarks that a certain publisher has work available. You can also learn a great deal of professional information during casual conversations by asking questions that you might be embarrassed to ask in other contexts. For example, you might not want to betray your inexperience to a client by asking what they meant by slugging,* whereas you wouldn't feel as embarrassed posing the same question to another freelancer. Or it might be something more basic, like typemarking.

Of course another way of networking is to attend professional meetings, conventions, and seminars. Most of my colleagues who are interested in working on computer materials attend the various computer conventions held in New York throughout the year. These are good opportunities to exchange business cards and sometimes to distribute résumés.

If there's a professional association in your city (e.g., the Freelance Editorial Association in Boston), it's a good idea to become a member.

---

* Slugging is the process of checking for missing or duplicated lines during page proofreading. Slugging is accomplished by laying the left edge of the text on the galley proof beside the corresponding left edge of the text on the page proof, and making sure they match line for line.

They are excellent sources of professional information and networking. For example, the Editorial Freelancers Association meets monthly, as do its medical writing, computers, trade nonfiction, and public relations affinity groups. All of these meetings are open to both members and nonmembers, though the latter are charged a small entrance fee. These meetings are an excellent way to meet other freelancers and potential clients and, in the case of the affinity groups, to exchange information in a tightly focused area of interest.

To summarize, here is a list of the main techniques you can use to market yourself:

- Keep in touch with clients and colleagues by phone
- Read and respond to the want ads regularly
- Send out query letters on a regular basis
- Network by joining professional organizations and by attending conventions, seminars, and editing courses (for more information on courses, you might want to take a look at *69 Workshops for Copy Editors* from *Copy Editor* newsletter, or the *1993/94 Directory of Publications Resources*, or see Appendix C3).

PLACES TO LIST

At the beginning of the chapter I mentioned that one way of finding clients is through directories. By the same token, listing yourself in directories is another way to market yourself. For example, several of my friends list themselves in LMP (it's free, if you can supply references), and have actually gotten calls from these listings. You can also advertise your availability in such trade magazines as *Publishers Weekly* and *Adweek*.

Over the years I have listed in *Freelancers of North America: 1984–5 Marketplace* and *Who's Who in Writers, Editors & Poets*, both of which went to libraries and were offered to publishers as well. Listing in both of these directories was free, though it was suggested that I buy a copy. I once got a call as a result of my listing in the North America book.

Association directories are also excellent places in which to list. Usually membership in the association will get you a free listing, as it does, for example, in the directories of both EFA and the Freelance Editorial Association. Most publishers have copies of these directories.

Check your library for other appropriate directories. Listing is usually free, because they hope you'll buy a copy. A cautionary note on fees: Several years ago there was a company in Buffalo, New York, that maintained a list of freelancers which it made available to companies or individuals who needed editorial workers. It cost a substantial amount to register, and I'm sure the publisher also paid an access fee. I would suggest that you check out such places carefully before you plunk down your money.

The problem with these listings, especially in directories, is that the prospective client has very little to go on in making a choice. That's why most in-house editors tend to prefer referrals when hiring new freelancers. In fact, freelancers get a substantial number of their jobs through word of mouth, which is why networking is so important.

Being a beginning freelancer is a lot like being the new kid in school: the more people you get to know, the more you get known, and as you go along, you acquire a certain reputation (see Chapter 6). Reputation is the key factor when other freelancers are trying to think of people to recommend to their clients. I recently spent the better part of a morning trying to track down the names of a few proofreaders to pass on to a publisher. Many of the possibilities were supplied to me by friends whom I'd called to see if *they* were interested in the job. These referrals were made not because my friends were familiar with the people's work, but because they had met the people and judged them reliable and professional. If these freelancers hadn't engaged in some form of networking, we never would have known of them or their editorial capabilities.

As another example, McGraw-Hill was my first book publisher client. After I had done several jobs for them, I received a call from an editor at another house. During the course of our conversation, she told me that she had been given my name by my boss at McGraw. Since that time, practically all of my new clients have come to me by such referrals. I even got one client partly because I'm mentioned in the acknowledgment section of Karen Judd's *Copyediting.*

Now that we've investigated some of the ways by which you can find clients—or they can find you—we're ready to move on to the business of freelancing.

NOTES

1. Ursula Brennan, "The Art of Collaboration," *EFA Newsletter,* vol. XVI, no. 4, April-May 1992.
2. *EFA Newsletter,* vol. 5, no. 5, May-June 1981, p. 12.

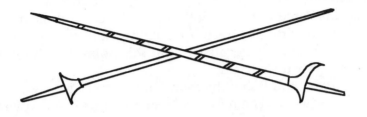

FREELANCING AS A BUSINESS

6

If there's one point that I want to emphasize above all others, it is this: Freelancing is a business. One of the first stories I heard after I started freelancing was about "the freelancer who couldn't." Over the years I've encountered several variations on this theme, one quite recently. Whatever form it takes, it's the project editor's worst nightmare

Once upon a time, the story goes, in the days before every writer had a computer (ca. 1976), a certain freelance copyeditor was hired to do a particular job. The next day the messenger delivered the package containing the manuscript (the only copy, alas!), instructions on how to fulfill the job, a supply of editorial flags, and a bill form. The freelancer gazed upon the manuscript, gulped, and said, "This is more than I expected. There's no way I can do this job." He then opened the bottom drawer of his desk, dropped in the entire pile of papers, and went out for a walk to consider what to do. Feeling overwhelmed and fearful, he finally decided to do nothing. A couple of days later, the editor called to find out if the job had arrived. "Yes," said the freelancer. (What else could he say? "It got lost in the messenger?") "How's it look?" the editor asked. "OK." "Any problem with the deadline?" "Nope." Those were the last words the editor heard from the freelancer. When the deadline came and went with no sign of the job, the editor called, but got no answer. She kept calling. Nothing. She tried sending a telegram. Nothing. Finally, in desperation, she went to the freelancer's address but no one answered the door. Both the freelancer and the manuscript had disappeared without a trace. We can only hope that the author had kept a copy of his work, because it is at this point that the storyteller and memory draw the curtain.

While you may think that the moral of this story is "always make a copy," Aesop says no. The moral is "when you realize you've made a mistake, call your editor."

Confessing your mistakes to those who hire you may not be a problem for *you*, but it is for some people. Whatever the reason—unwillingness to disappoint or to go back on one's word once it's given, a deepseated need to avoid confrontation, fear of not being hired again by the client or of getting a bad reputation, or just plain wimpiness—it must be overcome.

Not only was the freelancer's action a poor business practice, but it's the kind of response that hurts the reputation of editorial freelancing in general. Now let's take a look at some more constructive ways to act in the kinds of situations that typically confront freelancers.

REPUTATION

Although reputation is not, strictly speaking, a business practice, it would be extremely difficult to conduct a business without a good "rep," particularly in such a highly competitive profession as editorial freelancing. If we consider the freelancer in the story, it's obvious that he damaged his reputation by behaving the way he did. Few editors who knew of his actions would risk hiring him, but if he'd admitted his mistake at the outset, his client would have been understandably annoyed, but she might eventually have hired him again for other projects. The community of freelancers is relatively small—when I started I knew most of the technical copyeditors in New York either personally or by reputation—and word gets around fairly quickly, partly because editors move so frequently between houses, as well as from staff to freelance and back.

Instead of dwelling on the things a freelancer can do to damage his or her reputation, however, let's consider some of the ways in which a freelancer can build and bolster a reputation. Here is a list. While points 1, 2, 4, and 7 need no further comment, points 5, 6, and 8 are covered in the subsections that follow the list. Point 3 is discussed throughout the book, but especially in Chapter 5.

1. Meet deadlines. It is very important that you meet
    your deadlines, because nothing can harm your
    reputation more than constantly being late. One way
    to keep to the schedule is to begin work as soon as
    you receive the job. The temptation here is to look at
    the due date, which may be four to six weeks away,
    and say to yourself that that's more time than you
    need. If you postpone, you're sure to wake up one
    morning with less time than you need. Rushing to
    finish a job hurts quality. Most freelancers will tell
    you that a deadline focuses the mind incredibly,
    though self-imposed deadlines aren't always as
    effective as client-imposed ones, while open-ended
    jobs encourage postponement.

    Of course there will be occasions when you legiti-
    mately can't make your deadline. In such cases, you
    should call your client at least a week ahead to request
    a short extension, usually a day or two. The best such
    situation is when the deadline falls on a Thursday or
    Friday, because you can then ask for an extension over
    the weekend. Usually there's enough flexibility in the
    schedule to accommodate your request.

2. Do top-quality work. We all have standards that we
    work toward. Mine were ingrained by my first job in
    publishing, where the house style was all-important,
    and even a misplaced comma was corrected in page
    proofs. It's sometimes not possible to maintain these
    standards, however, because the client's schedule or
    budget or both—and hence instructions—won't
    allow it. In those instances, just do the best you can
    under the circumstances.

3. Behave (and dress) in a professional way.

4. Keep abreast of industry trends and as up to date
    with the appropriate technology as possible. This
    does not mean that you have to own the latest
    answering machine or fax—or even the newest
    WordPerfect upgrade—only that you should keep
    current enough to stay competitive. Don't be afraid
    to modernize your equipment when it's clear that
    you will lose clients if you don't.

5. Subcontract when you've overcommitted.

6. Ask for professional acknowledgment when appropriate.
7. Take pride in your work.
8. Don't underrate yourself.

Subcontracting

There are two types of situations in which editorial freelancers may consider subcontracting: (1) when they take on more work than they can handle alone, and (2) when a publisher hires a freelancer as a project editor, usually for one particular job.

When freelancers find themselves with an excess of work, it is perfectly all right to hire another freelancer to help out, as long as it's okay with the client. One way the indexer mentioned in Chapter 2 could handle so many jobs at once was that she hired a young man to do the scut work, like alphabetizing the index cards (this was before there were computer programs for indexing). Or you might want a freelancer to do one of the copyediting or proofreading jobs you can't handle.

Since it's your reputation that's at stake when you subcontract, you will want to find someone good who will work for a dollar or two less an hour than the client is paying you, and check that person's work before sending the job back to the client. This last is the main reason I have never subcontracted work: if I don't have time to do the project, I probably won't have time to make sure the completed work is up to my standards. In addition, you stand to lose money on the deal, since the time you spend checking the work is worth more than the difference between your fee and what you pay the other freelancer.

Still, many freelancers find subcontracting a satisfactory way of dealing with periods of overload or helping a client when they already have as many projects as they can handle.

Professional Acknowledgment

You can see an example of what I mean by "professional acknowledgment" if you turn to the copyright page of this book, where you will find the copyeditor and the indexer (the same person, in this instance) listed. Generally, when such acknowledgment is given, the list will include the sponsoring or acquisitions editor, the in-house project editor, and the book designer, but not the freelance copyeditor and/or indexer.

It is important to understand the distinction between being acknowledged by the author in the preface and being acknowledged by the publisher on the copyright page. Prefaces usually cite the names of numerous individuals who aided the author in the preparation of the book before it was submitted to the publisher, whereas the copyright page is a more appropriate place to acknowledge those persons involved in the development and production of the book, including freelancers as well as in-house personnel.

There are those who feel that asking for and receiving such credit is unprofessional. But why is it any less professional for a freelance copyeditor or indexer to be listed on the copyright page than it is for the production editor and the book designer?

A number of years ago, the Editorial Freelancers Association polled many of the major publishers to see which of them would agree to give a freelancer such professional acknowledgment. The answers to this survey revealed several interesting points:

> Some trade nonfiction publishers would do it, but most would not.

> No such acknowledgment would be given for works of fiction, perhaps because fiction is created by its author "out of nothing" except some research and a whole lot of imagination, while nonfiction might be said to be the arrangement of facts and/or occurrences already in evidence. A more likely explanation is that, in the case of fiction, it's inappropriate for the author to share credit in any way with a professional helper other than the librarian (often acknowledged in the Preface) who facilitated his or her research.

> No one wanted to acknowledge proofreaders in this way—a policy for which many proofreaders were grateful, because too many errors can be introduced between galleys and bound book.

> Generally, only college textbook publishers favored the idea—in fact, several already had such a policy in place. Their only caveat was that the freelancer had to request the citation, and the publisher had to agree that the job done warranted it.

> Some professional journals will include the freelancer's name on their masthead.

In support of this type of professional acknowledgment, Carolyn Smith, an editorial consultant specializing in textbook development, wrote the following in a 1988 issue of *Publishers Weekly:* "Formal acknowledgment enhances the careers of editorial professionals and provides information to those who might need similar services on another project."[1]

Smith then goes on to say, "Rather than it being considered unprofessional for editorial personnel to expect credit for their contributions, it should be recognized that the policy of not granting credit is unprofessional."[1]

It would therefore seem prudent from a professional standpoint for editorial freelancers to routinely request such acknowledgment, except in cases where they don't wish to have their name associated with a particular book.

Underrating Yourself

How can underrating oneself be harmful to an editorial freelancer's reputation? After all, anyone can feel uncertain when faced with a new challenge, such as when a copyeditor is offered a job involving the responsibilities of a freelance production supervisor, or a person doing simple word processing is asked to edit a book using a new electronic editing system. The trick is to know when such challenges can be turned into career-enhancing opportunities.

Unfortunately, many freelancers express their fears by accepting jobs and/or rates that aren't up to the level of their skills and experience. Not only does doing this harm their reputations but it's also a poor business practice.

Which is not to say that, when work is scarce, freelancers should refuse a job because the rate offered is less than the rate they usually charge. Taking such a job—say, for a small print shop or a mass market paperback publisher—is often a matter of survival. What I am saying is don't make it a general practice, because, as we'll see in Chapter 7, when freelancers undercharge or consistently work for less-than-market rates, potential well-paying clients may wonder if these freelancers undersell themselves because their abilities are below standard. If they come to this conclusion, they'll look elsewhere for freelance assistance.

PROFESSIONAL BEHAVIOR

Professional behavior is too broad a subject to be covered in a few pages, so I'll just hit the high spots here. Most of it is common sense anyway.

Keep regular office hours. Usually in-house editors have to assign their projects in a hurry and before noon. Most of the time, if you're not there when they call, you don't get the job. There are occasions, however, when you do have some leeway. For example, I came home one evening a few years ago to find the following message on my answering machine: "Trumbull, this is ———, at Scribner. I'm calling to ask if you'd be interested in copyediting Michener's introduction to our Hemingway book. If you could call me back tomorrow morning, Friday, I'd appreciate it. I need to assign it early tomorrow morning. Thanks." Imagine how I'd have felt if I'd missed *that* job!

But since most freelancers are in the business because of the freedom of the lifestyle, not everyone is going to follow this practice; for example, there's the freelancer who works between 1 P.M. and 6 P.M.; or the one who works Monday, Wednesday, and Friday 10 A.M. to 1 P.M., 8 P.M. to 9:30 P.M., 11 P.M. to 1 A.M., depending on the volume of work (if you have kids, you may recognize this schedule). Then there's the freelancer in a southwestern city who works at night, which means she often finishes jobs at 3 or 4 A.M. To enable her to deliver the finished work in the morning without her having to sacrifice her sleep, she and her clients have worked out some ingenious delivery systems. One leaves her car unlocked so the package can be left inside. Others have designated locations on their porches where she can leave the work. Even though she's making deliveries around 5 A.M., she doesn't try to mask her movements. This way she figures curious neighbors won't call the police. The system has been working successfully for the last few years—and not one job has been lost! Who could say the same for all of the so-called overnight delivery services?

In spite of the variations in their work schedules, most freelancers make themselves available Monday to Friday between 9 A.M. and 5 P.M. If you polled a group of freelancers about their hours, however, the most typical response would be, "Hah! Whatever it takes!"

Don't go to a client's place of business without first making an appointment, and when you do go, dress in a businesslike manner (see Chapter 5).

Keep up with technology as it affects publishing by reading such publications as *Publishers Weekly*, newspapers (for articles on new developments in computer technology, such as erasable CDs), and computer magazines. This way you can upgrade your hardware and software to stay current with the changing needs of your clients.

Be flexible. Successful freelancers will tell you that flexibility is the key to their success. After you gain some experience, it's not too difficult to edit any manuscript, whether or not you understand the subject matter. (With most specialized areas, such as law or psychology, it's a good idea to have a dictionary for that field so you can check spellings and usage.) One advantage of working on a wide range of topics is that the variety will help keep you from getting bored. You may want to take a mix of long- and short-term projects for the same reason.

Do what's asked of you, by which I mean don't copyedit when your assignment is proofreading or rewrite when you've been hired to edit. Also, there's no such thing as a stupid question, so when in doubt, ask.

Maintain your standards, no matter how boring or routine the job. In other words, don't become careless because you think the job isn't worth the effort or the client won't know the difference. Freelancers who maintain high standards become known throughout the industry and can usually count on steady, high-paying work.

When it comes to business, don't be ruled by your emotions. One way to avoid this is to keep your business relationships strictly professional (see the last section of this chapter). Perhaps this is a good place to remind you that clients are people, with their own idiosyncracies, personalities, and problems. Therefore, don't take it amiss when they don't sound "up" or enthusiastic. I have one client who always answers the phone as though I'm the last person in the world she wants to talk to. Confronted by an editor like this, some freelancers get insecure and defensive. In the case of my client, I've discovered that she doesn't sound that way because of my performance—she's like that with everybody. So don't jump to conclusions. If your work is unsatisfactory, you'll know about it soon enough.

If you take a temporary in-house freelance job, show up on time and follow the dress code. Be cheerful and accommodating, but not so much so that you feel taken advantage of. We talk more about this later in the chapter.

To summarize: Be reliable, accessible, and enthusiastic. But above all, have confidence in yourself.

RECORDKEEPING

The basis of every successful business is good recordkeeping. Before your eyes glaze over, let me add its equally important corollary: *document everything*. Although both of these statements may seem self-evident, it's worthwhile to expand on them a bit.

There are several types of records that you will want to keep:

> A time sheet (also see Chapter 8)
> A diary
> A work log
> Files on each project
> A spreadsheet or other system for recording income
> and expenses
> Receipts

Although the majority of your records will be helpful at tax time (or during a tax audit, if such should befall you), some will also help you keep track of your work flow. Even though, in the next three subsections, I use my methods to illustrate the processes, they are not the only ways to keep these records. The best way is the way that works best for you.

The Time Sheet

The time sheet can be defined as a daily record of billable hours. It can be any size or shape and can take any form that suits you—even notes on a calendar. I use pages from a three-by-five-inch note pad, taking a fresh sheet for each new project. At the top write the name of the client, an abbreviation of the book's title, the type of work (copyediting, proofreading, etc.), and the page number, since you will sometimes go through more than one page per project. On the first day, write its abbreviation (i.e., Mon., Tues., Wed.) and under it the date. Next to the day, write the time you start work on that project (e.g., 915). When you take a break, draw a dash and record the time you stopped working (e.g., 1045). After the break, write down your starting time under the previous starting time, and continue in this fashion until you stop work for the day. Finally, add up the hours and write the total under the last entry (e.g., 5¼ hrs). The total should also be entered in the diary (see the following subsection). Continue in this fashion until the project is finished.

When the client allows partial billing (see Chapter 8 for more on this subject), and you've added up the total hours for a designated period, write "Billed 0/0/00" (the date of the invoice) and circle it at that point on the time sheet so you'll know what hours you've already billed for when it comes time to bill again. When the project is complete or where multiple pages are used, when both sides of the page are full, clip the page to your file copy of the bill form(s).

The time sheet rarely has any other purpose than to keep track of the number of hours worked. I suppose a client could ask you to prove that you spent as many hours as you claim you did on a project, but I've only heard of one instance where it happened (see Chapter 8). Usually when they think you've overcharged they pay the bill and never call you again. I have only had one client that demanded I accept less than I billed, and that was a small publisher that wasn't happy with the job I did. They said they had to have the job done over and they felt they shouldn't have to pay twice for the same work. Since they considered me the cause of this duplication of effort, they wanted me to share the cost. I accepted the reduction, but was told later by other freelancers that I hadn't behaved very professionally. What I should have done, they said, is insist on full payment of my bill. This would have been a better business practice because, by backing down and agreeing to the client's demand, I compromised my professional status by accepting less than what I thought I was worth.

The Diary

For my diary, I use a Week At-a-Glance appointment book, called the Business Reminder. Although this particular version of the Week At-a-Glance book is difficult to find, you can see from the sample page in Figure 1 that its concise format is perfect for our purposes. The figure also shows the kinds of entries that should be made:

1. A summary statement of the total hours worked on each project on any given day
2. Work-related long-distance telephone calls (some freelancers keep a separate phone log) and fax transmissions
3. Photocopying and postage expenses
4. Business-related meals, including the name(s) of the participants, where they work, and the nature of the business discussed (the same information should be written on the back of the credit card receipt)
5. Business supplies purchased

In your diary the expenses should be circled in red so that they can be easily identified. Volunteer activities for a trade association, while not tax deductible (hence, the cost of the meal is *not* circled), are part of your professional life.

The diary should be maintained on a daily basis and should be as complete as possible. While the IRS doesn't consider it a primary source, if you're ever audited, it will help you substantiate your legitimate business expenses. Sometimes the auditor will ask to see it, for example, if you've claimed a meal of less than $25 for which you didn't keep the receipt.

Equally important, the diary will help you track your work flow, since you should also enter the arrivals and departures of your projects or portions thereof. If a client calls to ask where certain chapters are, a quick look at the diary (or work log) can tell you (1) if you received them, (2) when they arrived, and (3) when you returned them to the publisher. The diary will also tell you the time you sent the package and by what method—type of mail or messenger—which you probably

JANUARY
S	M	T	W	T	F	S
			1	2	3	4
5	6	7	8	9	10	11
12	13	14	15	16	17	18
19	20	21	22	23	24	25
26	27	28	29	30	31	

from **JANUARY 27**

MONDAY, JAN. 27 27/339	TUESDAY, JAN. 28 28/338	WEDNESDAY, JAN. 29 29/337
650 - started work on Preppy copyediting (worked 4 hours)	630 - started work on Preppy copyediting (worked 5 hours)	615 - started work on Preppy copyediting (worked 4 1/4 hours)
10 - Called author at UC Davis in California (916) -	1030 - went to post office to put batch in Express mail ($19.95)	1035 - returned Fran Fumps garden's call - agreed to take new project - start first of the month - hope the schedule holds -
230 - Emily Editor called from Preppy with another project after this one - I said yes -	1230 - met Fran Fump garden for lunch - she's an editor at McGraw and we talked about freelance work ($45.95, including tip; $2.50 trans.)	
		130 - met EFA panel for lunch - discussed next month's program - ($95.60 plus $12. tip)
A - started work on Z - Prop proofreading (worked 4 hours)		
5 - ran out to copy shop to do xeroxing of Preppy project ($25.95)	3 - stopped at stationery store for supplies ($15.49)	530 - Women's City Club for EFA meeting on "Why a Computer and a Fax?" good discussion - Home by 9 -
6 - went to Y for workout - part of doctors recommended program -	430 - went to doctor for checkup ($25; plus $2.50 trans.)	

← Clip for Current Week

Figure 1. Sample page of a diary.

won't have recorded in the work log. You'll also be able to tell at a glance how many hours you work in a day or a week; this will enable you to determine whether there's enough time in your schedule to accept additional jobs.

The Work Log

Figure 2 shows my way of keeping a work log, but it can also be maintained on a computer. As the figure shows, the work log is a chronological record of projects coming to the freelancer and going back to the client. Mine also includes a record of my billing, but again this can instead be kept as a separate file on your computer.

Do not jumble up your clients, but maintain separate records for each. I keep my work log in alphabetical order by client in a small ring binder. This way each client is easy to locate, and I can quickly see what work I have on hand, what parts of the project I've returned, and when I can expect payment on outstanding bills. For example, I know that Preppy Publishers takes two weeks to pay, and that Z-Prop (a total-concept house) takes about four weeks, depending on how promptly it gets paid by *its* client. Thus, a glance at when the bills were submitted will tell me approximately what my future cash flow will be like. It will also alert me to overdue payments, so I can call the editor to see what's happened. Sometimes the person signing checks has been out of the office unexpectedly, but more often the bill has gotten lost. In the latter case, the editor will sometimes walk my bill down to the accounting department. On some occasions I've then received my check within a few days. But don't count on this happening, as not all accounting departments are so accommodating. The bill will be resubmitted, but you may have to wait another cycle before they'll write the check.

The work log does not contain a record of the projects you've committed to in the future, only those that are currently in-house. I used to be very good at tracking my work flow in my head. Then one day about two years ago a favorite client—Client X—called and I agreed to do a fairly simple job for them starting a few weeks hence. Since, as we'll see in Chapter 10, promised jobs have a way of evaporating, I've formed the habit of accepting other work as a safeguard. Somehow forgetting about my promise to Client X, I kept on accepting work up to my limit. The day the job arrived from Client X, I sat there stunned, with the box sitting on the table in front of me. For several minutes I couldn't figure out why it was there—what was in the box? Had someone sent me unsolicited work? Had someone made a mistake? I had just about decided to call for an explanation when I dimly recalled accepting the job. Because

3.

Preppy (1994)

11/1/94 - 11/29/94 - <u>Food for the Nineties: New</u>
<u>Strategies for Home Cookery and</u>
<u>Restaurant Cuisine</u>, by Mett & Sheff
Chapters 1-9 (406 pages), Glossary (6 pp),
Selected Reading (3 pp), Preface (5 pp),
Forward (3 pp), TOC (6 pp), plus 218 figures
and captions (13 pp)

11/15/94 - Chapters 1-4 to Preppy (203 pp; 100 figs;
6 pp of captions)

11/15/94 - Billed $<u>324.00</u> for 20¼ hours @ $16/hr
(Rec'd   )

11/17/94 - 11/29/94 - <u>Food for the Nineties</u>, by
Mett & Sheff - Appendixes A-E (40 pp)

11/29/94 - Chapters 5-9, Frontmatter, Appendixes to
Preppy (266 pp, 118 figs, & 7 pages of captions)

11/29/94 - Billed $<u>424.00</u> for 26½ hours @ $16/hr
(Rec'd   )   plus $23.75 for Express mail -
Total Bill $<u>447.75</u>

Figure 2. Sample page of a work log.

it wasn't very time-consuming, I managed to juggle things so all my projects were handled on time, but the experience rattled me. It told me I needed to rethink my method of keeping track of my commitments. As a result, I now keep a three-by-five index card posted over my desk as a kind of appendix to my work log. On it I list all current and future jobs and their projected deadlines. As I complete a job, I cross it out with a highlighting pen. When the card is full, I make a new one.

The work log is one of the more important records you will be keeping, so be scrupulous about making entries as they occur. This way, you will have a current record to refer to should questions arise.

Financial Planning Programs

Perhaps you think that what you have read so far in this section smacks of sleeve garters, cuff guards, and green eye shades, and is reminiscent of someone perched on a high stool at a narrow desk scratching away on parchment with a quill pen. "What about computers and spreadsheets and all that other high-tech stuff we keep reading about?" you ask. Fair enough. Many freelancers do use such technological aids, but before we go any further, perhaps we should define some terms.

When most of us think about computer programs to help us keep track of our finances, we conjure up spreadsheets. But is a spreadsheet program really called for? According to the *Microsoft Press Computer Dictionary*, a spreadsheet is "an application program commonly used for budgets, forecasting, and other finance-related tasks."[2] But doesn't this sound like a program that is perhaps too powerful for a freelancer's simple needs? After all, all we really want is a place to dump deposits and expenses, a program that will give us totals when we ask for them. Isn't there something a little less elaborate?

Yes, there is: accounting software. As defined by *The Random House Personal Computer Dictionary*, accounting software is "a class of computer programs that perform accounting operations."[3] Accounting programs are of two main types: single-entry systems, or personal finance managers; and double-entry systems. Single-entry systems will help you automate both check writing and recordkeeping. Most freelancers, however, do not need the first function, but want more than the second offers.

This is why double-entry systems were developed. These programs have the ability to create a general ledger and to keep track of accounts receivable and accounts payable. This sounds like all I need, but if you think it's still not enough, there are more sophisticated systems that include functions for invoicing, inventory, time billing, payroll, and so forth.

Three of the more popular accounting programs are:

1. *Quicken*
2. *Microsoft Money*
3. *CA Simply Money*

For those freelancers who like to do their own taxes, there are several good tax programs, such as *Turbo Tax*. And, for those who still feel they want, or need, a spreadsheet rather than an accounting program, here are the names of three of the more popular ones:

1. *Excel for Windows*
2. *Microsoft Works*
3. *Lotus 1-2-3* (for DOS or for Windows)

Receipts

Since the first rule of recordkeeping is to document everything, you should form the habit of asking for a receipt for every business-related expense. Be sure the receipt contains the following information: date of purchase; name of the store; and total amount spent. The cash register at my local copy shop does not print its name on its receipts, but the employees will hand-stamp it upon request. When you pay by credit card, staple the cash register receipt to the credit card receipt.

Following is a list of most of the business-related expenses for which you should get receipts:

Office furniture and equipment
Office supplies
Reference or other work-related books
Photocopying
Postage, including overnight delivery services
Messengers
Transportation to and from clients, business meetings, or meals. In some areas, this may not be possible, but in New York, for example, most taxis will provide receipts upon request, although subways and buses do not. If, however, you need to take a commuter train or bus for business reasons, you should be able to get a receipt.
Meals and other entertainment. This category also includes food, wine, liquor, and other expenses incurred in preparing meals when entertaining a client in your home.

Business-related travel, including air and train fare, car rental, meals, and lodging. (Of course this and the previous listing are both subject to governmentally imposed restrictions when it comes to figuring the actual amount of the deduction.)

Files

From the start you will want to keep files in many categories, but as you continue you may wish to add other areas as well. As an aid to getting started, here is a brief list of some of the more obvious categories:

1. Correspondence
2. Contracts
3. Old work logs
4. Copies of newletters on editorial or other business-related subjects
5. Articles on editorial or other business-related subjects
6. Taxes
7. Each project

The first six entries in the list are self-explanatory, but the last item warrants further comment.

Set up a new file folder for each project you do. On the tab of each folder mark the following information (this is why I like the straight-cut-style folder): "File on <u>name of client, title of book, edition number,</u> and <u>author's (or authors') complete name(s).</u>" For example: File on Preppy, <u>Food for the Nineties: New Strategies for Home Cookery and Restaurant Cuisine</u> (2/e), by Gore Mett and Sue Sheff. When the job has been completed, I place the folder in the file cabinet, where all the project folders are arranged in alphabetical order by client's (not author's) name.

Each folder contains all the accumulated material related to that project, including copies of the style sheet; any queries made and answered during phone calls with the client; any list of special instructions from the client; any correspondence with the client, including cover letters, letters of agreement or other contracts, memos from both the client and me; other related material, such as design specs and sample pages that the client doesn't want returned; bill forms with time sheets attached; receipts from messengers; and photocopy and overnight mail receipts. If you have to include these latter receipts with your bill, keep photocopies of them.

I can think of at least three reasons why these files should be maintained. First and foremost, when an author likes the job a copyeditor did the first time around, it is fairly common for that author to ask the publisher to hire the same person for a subsequent edition or a new work. This can also happen when the client is happy with the job the freelancer did. Since the publisher might not keep such relevant material as the style sheet from the previous edition, the fact that you have a copy in your files will help you maintain special styling points in the new edition. Plus, you'll have the answers to many of the questions you might otherwise want to ask, such as whether you should correct the author's use of "which" and "that."

Second, the spelling, abbreviations, and acronyms lists on the style sheet can come in handy in a number of contexts. For example, I edit several journals on physics and astrophysics each year for one client, and I keep separate files for each job. This particular client has a style rule that all abbreviations and acronyms must be spelled out at their first occurrence in each paper in the volume; for example, "weakly interacting massive particle" (WIMP). The next time I'm editing manuscripts, I might not be able to find this acronym in my reference books, but if I look at the previous style sheets, chances are I'll find it spelled out there. Or I could be copyediting a book on particle physics for a different client, come across the same acronym, and be able to find it on that style sheet.

Third, you may want to refer to these files for other reasons. For example, when an author writes to the publisher to compliment the copyeditor, the in-house editor will often forward a copy to the freelancer. I have a copy of one such letter from a Nobel laureate that I like to bring out on occasion to show friends or clients.

Many freelancers purge old files every few years to make room in their file drawers for new ones. When they do, they store the old files in cardboard cartons somewhere else in the house. Years ago a freelancer told me he'd just packed a bunch of old files away in a closet when he received a call asking him to copyedit the latest edition of a book whose file he had just sealed in that carton.

Of course it's conceivable that in the future these files will be maintained on computer disks or other kinds of storage devices. In the meantime, though, it's a good business practice to follow the Collier brothers'* dictum: Save everything.

---

* Two wealthy reclusive brothers who lived in New York City. When they died in 1947, their bodies were discovered in a house crammed full of piles of old newspapers and magazines, plus cartons filled with all manner of stuff. No, they weren't freelance editors!

CONTRACTS

There are essentially three types of contracts you will be concerned with as an editorial freelancer: the letter of agreement; a similar document for when you take a temporary in-house job; and the work-for-hire contract.

The Letter of Agreement

A sample letter of agreement appears in Figure 3. This is a document that you should create after accepting any job over the phone. Unfortunately, although many freelancers follow this practice, too many others do not. Don't be concerned that you will alienate your client if you present him or her with a letter of agreement. There is nothing in it that suggests that you don't trust the person, as long as you stick to the simple facts of the case. In fact, sending one will enhance your professional image.

As you can see from the figure, a letter of agreement is a simple restatement of the things discussed and agreed to when a client calls with a job offer. Not all such letters will be as detailed as this one is, but all should be written in a similar style and format.

The point of these letters is to codify as many details as possible in case disagreements arise later on. This is especially true in the case of long-term projects, such as a manuscript of 1500 to 2000 pages, when memory may dim as the job progresses. While the editor may have told you to make *data* plural (as it should be) during your initial conversation, three weeks later, having reviewed the first batch of copyedited manuscript, she may have forgotten what she said. If you don't have this and other style choices documented, you may find yourself in an uncomfortable position, not to mention having to donate the time necessary to correct the pages you've turned since completing the last batch.

As an adjunct to the letter of agreement, the client will usually include a letter of instruction with the project, detailing special style points to be followed while editing the manuscript. Sometimes an entry or two will be made on the style sheet as well (see Appendix B for a sample). Your instructions won't always be this complete, however. I have worked for some editors who write cover letters that say no more than thanks for taking on the project, a description of what's enclosed, my copyediting rate, a deadline for each batch, and an invitation to call with any questions.

Some other points that might be included in a letter of agreement are the frequency with which the freelancer will submit his or her

Edith Editor
Preppy Publishers, Ltd.
6060 Fifth Avenue
New York , NY 10000
October 29, 1993

Dear Ms. Editor:

This letter is to confirm the particulars of our telephone conversation this morning concerning a cook book of approximately 420 pages, plus 218 figures. From the way you described the preparation of this manuscript, I understand that a medium copyedit is all that's required. Also, along with the copyediting, I am to do the following:

1. Turn the Table of Equivalents in Chapter 50 into an appendix and add it to the Table of Contents (TOC).
2. Create a log of all the color art.
3. Delete all second- and third-level heads from the TOC.
4. Check internal numbering and cross-references, as the chapters have been reorganized.
5. Prepare a separate sheet of figure legends.
6. Make sure all the temperatures are in °F; it is not necessary to add conversions.
7. Make sure all recipes include instructions for both microwave and conventional ovens.
8. I do not need to copyedit the art; just read it for typos and/or consistency with the text.
9. Edit the Bibliography according to *Chicago*.
10. Check permissions.

I understand that I am to return the manuscript in two batches of approximately equal length, one on November 15, 1993, and the second on November 29, 1993. I will include an invoice with each batch, at the agreed-upon rate of $18/hour.

If you agree that the contents of this letter are an accurate summary of our conversation this morning, please sign below and return one copy to me, and keep one for yourself.

I am looking forward to working with you on this project.

Sincerely,

Frieda Freelancer

_____

(Edith Editor)

_____

Figure 3. Sample letter of agreement.

invoices; when invoices will be paid, plus a stipulation of interest that will be charged by the freelancer if payment is late; and a cancellation fee for projects that are terminated either before they begin or after they've commenced. To my knowledge, the last two items are not current practice in the New York publishing community, although both are recommended by the Freelance Editorial Association in Cambridge, Massachusetts. On the other hand, most magazines pay their writers a "kill fee" if a story is canceled or not used after it's been agreed upon. I'm not sure how a publisher would react, for example, if you included a small interest charge for an overdue bill (for more on this, see Chapter 8), but if more freelancers attempted to protect themselves in these ways, changes in current practice might occur.

The In-house Contract

Although I don't include a sample in-house contract here, following is a list of subjects that might be covered by such a contract:

1. A statement of where the work will be performed
2. The actual days and hours the freelancer will work
3. The number of hours per week the freelancer will work
4. The hourly rate, the intervals at which bills will be submitted, and a provision for charging interest for late payments
5. The duration of the project
6. An agreement that an employer-employee relationship is not being created, and that the freelancer is therefore free to work for other clients
7. A termination agreement

Here are a few more general points about working in-house, though these won't necessarily be included in the contract.

Most part-time in-house freelancers follow the same office hours as do the regular staff, that is, 9 A.M. to 5 P.M., with time off for lunch. (Some legal proofreading and word processing jobs are at night. When this happens, the employer will often provide dinner at a good restaurant and limousine or taxi service to your home when the night's work has been completed.) Therefore you'll probably be asked to only work two or three days a week, because if you log thirty hours or more a week, they are supposed to consider you on staff and provide certain benefits. Working in-house therefore could jeopardize your status as a freelancer in the eyes of the IRS. (Check Chapter 9 for more on this.)

I know a freelancer—call him Bob—who works steadily for a publisher of professional journals. Although Bob only goes in once a week, the company has provided him with desk space and two file drawers. A few years ago the company had three other freelancers who came in on an irregular basis, and also had office space. Then, because the IRS was getting strict about such arrangements, the three other freelancers joined the staff and started collecting benefits, although they still only went in two or three days a week, and at least one continued to work for another client occasionally. What about Bob? Why wasn't he forced out of the freelance life as well? The reason was that he could show that he had enough other regular clients that he couldn't be considered an employee of the company. Of course, if this had not been the case, chances are he would have stopped working for this publisher so that he could continue freelancing.

This provision was designed to protect the freelancer. Otherwise a publisher could fire all its editorial staff and hire freelancers to come in to do the work, the only difference being that now they wouldn't have to provide benefits. Since you're going to have to pay for your health insurance and other benefits yourself, however, why work for one company at, say, $20 an hour, when you could work for several clients for the same rate? The latter arrangement makes better economic sense.

Since you're a worker without portfolio when you work in-house, the first thing you want to establish is who you report to and what your exact duties are. That way, if someone tries to assign you work, you can politely refer them to your boss, who should be able to handle the situation. This is not to say that you should never do small chores for other staffers; only that the request should come through your boss. Also, if someone comes to you with a request, and you have the time and inclination to say yes, it's still best to run it by your boss.

You should be assigned a regular workstation, phone, and typewriter or given access to a computer. Of course, since you're an outsider, be prepared to be moved around as the ebbs and flows of personnel in the office require. If you feel that you've been given inadequate space to work in, talk it over with your boss. Perhaps something else can be worked out, though probably not at that instant.

Dress in a manner similar to your fellow workers. In other words, don't wear jeans if the rest of the staff wears jackets and ties (for men) or dresses (for women). Personally, I'm more comfortable wearing a tie and shined shoes, even in situations where the attire is more casual.

The company should provide all the supplies you need to accomplish the job. If for some reason you are required to purchase some items on your own, the company should reimburse you. (Remember to get receipts.)

You should be given access to the photocopying machine and the fax if your duties require their use. If you're working on an editorial assignment, chances are they will.

Be cheerful.

Don't allow yourself to be pulled into office politics and gossip. If you give in to this temptation, you'll likely make more enemies than friends, which could cost you future clients as well as harm your professional image.

The sad news is that not everyone working for the company will regard freelancers very highly. I once overheard a senior staff member say in reference to me, "He's just a freelancer," as though relegating me to the level of the custodial department or cleaning service. Don't buy into this. You've been hired to do a job because you possess skills and/or knowledge that they need in order to accomplish a particular job. This is why I recommend that freelancers who take temporary in-house jobs call themselves "editorial consultants" or just "consultants." It's a slightly classier title than "copyeditor" or "proofreader," and may make you feel better about yourself and why you're there. But whatever you call yourself, if this put-down attitude persists to the point where it begins to bother you, discuss it with your boss. If that doesn't help, you can always quit, but if you do, be sure your boss knows the reason why.

Of course, such prejudice is rare. The remark just mentioned was the only instance that occurred during the year or so the job lasted. The vast majority of in-house editors hold freelancers in high regard; most have been freelancers themselves at one time or another during their careers. I only bring up the subject because, like many other prejudices, it's there in a small minority of people, and you should be prepared for it in case it crops up.

To summarize, having a formal contract is a good business practice, as it makes both parties aware of the specific terms of the agreement and lets them know where they stand. As with the letter of agreement, however, the only contract most freelancers have when they take an in-house job is verbal. Which is strange, since no contract of this nature should be objectionable to a client, as it's beneficial to both parties.

Work-for-Hire Contracts

The last of the three types of contracts that you'll come across as an editorial freelancer is the least desirable of the three, particularly if you're a magazine writer. In fact, various writers' organizations have, at one time or another, mounted campaigns against it—but without success. The reason the work-for-hire contract is held in such disregard is that by signing it you relinquish certain rights to the work performed. Therefore, if you're a writer working under work-for-hire, you sign over all rights of ownership to the company or person who hires you for a one-time set fee. In other words, you get, say, $500 and the company that hired you gets the pamphlet or whatever it is you've agreed to write. If this pamphlet becomes a best seller in, say, the pharmaceutical industry, you won't make a penny more from it than the $500 you contracted for originally. This is the same contract that gives large organizations ownership of patents on lucrative inventions made by company employees. Most businesses hiring writers for one-time writing projects routinely require the writer to sign the contract as a condition of employment.

While a work-for-hire contract can occasionally work against the writer, in many cases the work produced doesn't generate significant income. For an editor, however, it makes absolutely no difference if you sign such a contract. In fact, freelancers working for some publishers sign a work-for-hire clause when they sign their invoice. I don't object to this because it doesn't change my expectations; I never benefit financially from the future sales of any book or paper I edit. That's not the nature of the job, and I don't know of any editors who seriously want to change these parameters.

In the long run, your feelings about the work-for-hire contract will be shaped by the type of work you do. For example, people who write material for textbooks and the like find it a legitimate way to handle such assignments. If you're an editor/writer, the writer part may hate it, while the editor part will give it no thought.

CLIENT RELATIONSHIPS

Client relationships should be kept on a strictly professional level. This is not to say that you should be cold and calculating, or that you should suppress your natural friendliness when dealing with clients. But there is a difference between being friendly and encouraging close, personal relationships with the in-house editors you work for. The best way to keep from crossing this line is to establish good business practices at the outset and stick to them scrupulously.

This can be a difficult dictum to adhere to, however, mainly because we're human, which means that most of us are gregarious and social. Also, as freelancers, we are in an odd position in our relations with the in-house editors for whom we work: Although we're hired by them, we are also free agents. This means that, on occasion, editors will feel free to confide things to us that they wouldn't dream of telling their staff or their bosses. These confidences can be of a personal nature; more often, they will be work-related. Such sharing can quite naturally lead to the intimacy of close friendship. I think there are few freelancers who don't succumb at one time or another to this temptation.

But then the day comes when the in-house editor is told by a superior that our work on the last project wasn't up to standard, and that we should not be hired again. Or something happens in the friendship that causes a rift—perhaps a secret is told, an agreement isn't kept, or one party suddenly decides the relationship is too one-sided. Either way, we lose favored-freelancer status and suddenly we're not receiving the same volume of work, or perhaps our ex-friend begins spreading adverse rumors about our reliability or professionalism. All or any of this can have a negative effect on our careers, especially as we've been leaning heavily on that particular client for work.

The same admonition holds true for relations with authors and printers. For example, a number of years ago a small textbook publisher hired me to work on a college algebra book by an author who was particularly difficult to work with—what some would call a p.i.a. Somehow we worked well together—my editor said it was because I gave him everything he asked for, but I prefer to think it was because I could read his handwriting, a prerequisite for this author, who handwrote many of his Exercises sections. Whatever the reason, I soon became the official copyeditor for a whole series of books he wrote for the company.

Except one. I was too busy with other projects at the time to take it on, so the company hired another freelancer. About a month later I got a call from the author (he'd been given my home number during an earlier project). He said he couldn't work with the new freelancer, he hated the job that person was doing, so wouldn't I please take over?

This request presented me with a dilemma. In the first place, the author had broken one of the cardinal rules of publishing by approaching me directly, particularly in the middle of the editing process. But even if I'd been starving, from an ethical standpoint I could not have said yes. If I did, that would put the company in a difficult position, especially since it was satisfied with the job the other freelancer was doing. Also, I couldn't call the editor and tell him the author had called to ask me to take over the copyediting of his book, and that I'd agreed to do so. Nor could the author call and say he wanted to change copyeditors and knew I was free and willing to do it. So I said no. I did, however, proofread the galleys and pages, which mollified the author somewhat. As I said earlier, it's okay to be friendly, but hold the line against intimacy. If you're not careful, you can cross this line almost without being aware of it. It's tricky, so keep in mind what this chapter (and ultimately this book) is all about: editorial freelancing is a business, not a hobby; it's a profession, not an avocation. The only way you're going to succeed at it is to treat it in that light.

A WORD ON ACCOUNTANTS

Most freelancers think of accountants only in terms of taxes—how many deductions am I missing by not using an accountant?—but they can help in other areas of financial planning as well. On average, freelancers probably do their own taxes because they consider accountants a luxury. But freelancing is a *business,* and businesses should have an accountant.

There are several ways to find an accountant. The first and most obvious is to ask your friends and family for the names and phone numbers of *their* accountants. Another is to look in the Yellow Pages under Accountants—Certified Public, but this can be daunting, especially in a large city like New York. If you live in a metropolitan area, there may also be accountant referral services, which function the same way as those that put people in touch with doctors or dentists. Some accountants, especially new ones, advertise by direct mail.

If you choose an independent CPA rather than an accounting firm, try to find one whose practice focuses on small businesses, preferably with some clients who are in arts-related professions. That way you can be fairly certain that the person in question is up on the tax laws as they pertain to independent contractors.

Whatever method you use to find your accountant, it's important that you have an initial consultation in which you discuss such issues as:

1. Your business situation; that is, the type of work you do; your gross annual business income; what retirement funds, if any, you have; and the extent of your business deductions.
2. Other personal income and deductions; that is, income from stocks, bonds, annuities, or trusts; whether you itemize your deductions or take the standard deduction.

This discussion will help establish the amount and level of work involved. Of course you may want to explore other areas as well, but I think this list provides you with a base from which to start.

Fees will vary according to where you live, and according to whether you use a firm or an independent CPA. If the former, the standard billing rate (SBR) will be determined by one of several methods, usually based on a percentage of the accountant's salary. This means you can expect to be charged in the range of $40 to $60 an hour (unless you're working with senior staff, in which case the range would be $80 to $100 per hour) plus some kind of adjustment for overhead plus out-of-pocket expenses. This is only a rough estimate, however, because in the end it's the firm's policy that determines what the fee will be.

More normally, however, freelancers use independent CPA's who specialize in taxes. These accountants will use one of three methods to determine their fees:

1. *Hourly rates.* In this method, accountants charge between $125 and $250 an hour. The time covered includes consultation time, client time, and preparation time, all of which can take between 1½ and 5 hours.
2. *Flat rates.* Flat rates can vary between $125 and $250. However, since the flat rate is based on how much work is involved, the amount of time spent, and the client's ability to pay, this estimate could be $100 or more too low.
3. *By the form.* According to this method, the accountant charges a set amount per form plus a base charge plus a consultation fee (e.g., $12 + $100 + $25). As freelancers, we need to file a minimum of six or seven different federal tax forms (see Chapter 9), plus state and local forms, so you could expect a charge of $245 for 10 forms (6 federal, 2 state, 2 city). Of course if there are more forms involved, the price will be higher; if fewer forms, the cost will be less.

Now that we've reviewed the business side of freelancing, we're ready to move on to the subject of money. The following chapter therefore contains advice on how to establish and negotiate rates, as well as what you can expect in this area.

NOTES

1. Carolyn D. Smith, "Credit Where Credit Is Due," *Publishers Weekly*, June 10, 1988, p. 52.
2. *Microsoft Press Computer Dictionary* (2nd ed.), Microsoft Press, Redmond, Wash., 1994, p. 370.
3. Philip E. Margolis, *The Random House Personal Computer Dictionary*, Random House, New York, 1991, p. 6.

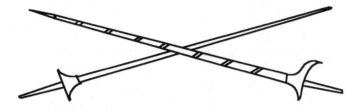

ALL ABOUT RATES

7

Although publishing has always had the reputation of paying its editorial workers low wages, it has managed to attract highly intelligent and dedicated editors. During my youth and before I became involved in the industry, I shared the common perception of editors as well-educated individuals from wealthy families who could afford to spend their days worrying about the niceties of grammar (are split infinitives ever acceptable? When do you use the serial comma?), style (*which* vs. *that, farther* vs. *further*), and typefaces (Baskerville, Craw Clarendon, or Goudy Old Style? Serif or sans serif?). With such interesting choices, I didn't see editors as being overly concerned about the size of their pay checks—a coupon could always be clipped or a dividend check counted upon to arrive in time to provide the necessities. Besides, it was a privilege to be able to spend one's days in such a quiet, contemplative, and highly civilized way.

After I started freelancing, I revised my picture somewhat. I began to see the freelancer and in-house editor as having a symbiotic relationship of a rather special nature. For example, if the freelancer was short of funds, she need only ask her "boss" if her check could be expedited. The in-house editor would then go to her friend in the accounting department and say, "Frieda Freelancer is one of my best freelancers and I'd like to keep her happy, so can you get her check out right away?" and it would be done. However, since the advent of huge conglomerates with accounting departments that are no longer familiar with the traditions of publishing and focused—one could almost say fixated—on the "bottom line," all that has changed. Nevertheless, even with its low rates, publishing has remained a top career choice for many bright young minds right out of college.

Still, it is interesting to speculate about why rates for editorial freelancing services remain comparatively low. In fact, a few years ago one large publishing company that was already paying the lowest rates in the industry *reduced* its copyediting rate for general nonfiction from $13 to $12 an hour.

One reason for this situation may be that, at the editorial level, publishing, and especially freelancing, is a female-dominated profession. In accordance with the conditions prevailing in all such professions the rates and salaries commanded by editors are lower than those paid for comparable work in male-dominated professions. Thus, if you decide you want to proofread for a bank or a large corporation, chances are you can make upwards of $30 per hour, while if you proofread for a major book publisher, you'll probably make no more than $18 per hour, and most likely $12.[1] In fairness, I should also point out that profit margins in publishing are considerably lower than in other industries—another reason payments for editorial services have traditionally been low. In fact, when a book's budget is made up, the amount set aside for copyediting and proofreading is the smallest piece of the pie, in spite of the importance of these functions to the book's quality and, thus, its sales.

DETERMINING YOUR RATE

Hourly versus Project Rates

"Which is better, project or hourly rates? An interesting answer to this old debate emerged from analysis of responses to the [EFA] Rates Survey.* The very high earners [more than $45,000 a year] universally praised project rates as more lucrative. The very low earners [less than $15,000 a year] tended to do worse working by the project and preferred to charge by the hour."[2]

The decision whether to charge by the project, the hour, the line, or the page is usually determined either by the type of work involved or

---

* Last published as such in 1991. In 1994, EFA started publishing the *Professional Practices Survey* instead. This survey is now scheduled to be published every two years.

by the client. Since charging by the line and the page are most often associated with indexing, the present discussion focuses on project and hourly rates.

In my experience project rates are associated more with writing or rewriting than with copyediting or proofreading. Since, however, you will occasionally be asked to estimate the total cost of a copyediting or proofreading project, this is a good skill to have. When determining the cost of a project, you first need to estimate the total number of hours it will take you to complete the task, then add in any incidental costs you think you will incur, plus a small margin. For example, suppose that you are being offered a job copyediting a manuscript that is 550 pages long, is not in overly bad shape (they say), and is nontechnical (straight text). Besides copyediting, they want you to code the various elements for the typesetter (these are not computer typesetting codes), check the table of contents against text, proofread the art, and edit the figure legends. There are no tables or references, but there is a ten-page bibliography and there are three appendixes, the latter to be shot (photographed with the art) rather than set. They want you to turn between eight and ten pages an hour (which is reasonable), so base your estimate on the slower time (eight pages):

$$550 \text{ pages} \div 8 \text{ pages/hour} = 68.75 \text{ hours},$$

add in a few extra hours for miscellaneous project-related tasks such as phone calls, going to the copy shop and/or post office, and making out your invoice, then multiply by the agreed-upon hourly rate:

$$72.75 \text{ hours} \times \$15/\text{hour} = \$1091.25.$$

Thus, your bid would be $1100.00.

If you get into the project and find that it's more complex than it first seemed, stop and call the client to discuss it. She may not be willing to pay more than your estimate and may therefore ask you to be less thorough than you think necessary. Or she may want to see a sample of what you're talking about before making a decision. Whatever the outcome, get it confirmed in writing, as we discussed in Chapter 6.

The process is the same for writing projects, only it takes a certain amount of experience to know how long it will take you to complete different types of assignments. One aid to determining how long previous projects of various kinds took you to complete is to keep detailed records. In these cases, the bid figure usually becomes the agreed-upon amount for the project. Therefore, if it takes you longer than you thought it would to complete the work, you have to absorb the difference. And, if it takes you less time, you get the excess, which is the main appeal for charging by the project rather than by the hour.

Most publishing houses pay by the hour and will ask for, or offer, an hourly rate. Since most general discussions of rates are carried on in terms of hourly rates, all of what follows presupposes the hourly rate.

The "True" Rate

Thus far I have usually cited a rate of $15 per hour for copyediting. This is because, although rates vary depending upon where you live, fifteen is a convenient number to multiply and divide by. Yet, neither this nor the fact that recently published statistics show that the average American earns about $15.50 per hour[3] should necessarily be construed as meaning that $15 per hour is the current going rate for copyediting. In New York, for example, many publishers are now paying higher hourly rates than that. But whatever rate is finally agreed upon, it is not what is actually being earned. For $15 per hour that figure is more like $9.25 per hour, a rate not commonly paid since, say, 1983!

That is your "true" rate.

How do I figure this? It's quite simple. Every in-house employee is paid 38 percent in benefits above the cost of his or her salary; for example, a production editor who is being paid $22,000 a year is really earning $30,360, or $22,000 x 0.38 = 8,360, or 22,000 + 8,360 = 30,360.

Therefore, in order to truly make $15 per hour you need to figure in the cost of your health insurance, one-half your Social Security tax (about 9 percent; freelancers pay the entire 18 percent—see Chapter 9), a paid vacation, paid sick days, and so on, which are not paid for you by an employer. Thus, 15 x 0.38 = 5.7, or to the nearest convenient number, $5.75. Therefore, in order to make $15 per hour, you would need to charge $20.75 per hour.

Thus we see that when the in-house editor is let go so that the company can save on overhead by using freelancers, that "overhead" doesn't disappear, but is shifted to the freelancer.[4]

Industry Rates

Although there is no such thing as standard industry rates for the various editorial functions, most publishing houses pay the same or similar rates for these specific tasks. This will be true, no matter where in the country you live. As an example, when I was working for Scribner in the days before it was acquired by Macmillan, I told the person who was hiring me that I had increased my rate from $12 to $15 per hour. He said he'd see what he could do. A little while later he called back, and said, in effect, "I just called the Copy Chiefs at three or four other trade houses that are the same size as we are, and they all told me they are paying their freelancers $12 per hour, so I'm afraid I can't give you more than that." Well, I liked the man and I enjoyed working for him and for Scribner, so I decided to accept their offer. I guess you could say that in this case I put personal satisfaction above professionalism, a practice I don't recommend, since it's not really a good business practice (cf. Chapter 6).

As was said earlier, rates vary according to where you live. It is therefore a common perception that if you live in an area with a low cost of living, you can survive well on a lower hourly rate. When looked at objectively, however, this proves not to be the case, for the simple reason that you will also have higher business costs. By "higher business costs" I mean that since most of your clients will be in other parts of the country or even the world, the costs of communicating with them by phone or by fax will be higher than if you lived in a large city, especially one that is also a publishing center. In addition, it will cost you more to travel to the libraries where the reference books you need are located and the hours and/or days when you can send overnight mail will not be as convenient as in a metropolitan area. These are but three examples of higher business costs in low-cost areas, but they give an idea of what I mean.

Even so, how can you find out what the going rate is? Perhaps the most effective way of finding what rate works best for you is to sit down and figure a business budget. Once you know how much it will take to run your freelance business plus provide you with sufficient income to live in the manner to which you've become accustomed, it is easy enough to determine your hourly rate. First, however, you need to know the daily rate, which you can find by dividing the amount of your business budget by the number of billable days in a year. To translate that figure into an hourly rate, simply divide it by eight, or the number of hours worked in a day.[4]*

Another way is offered by rate and salary surveys such as those published by the Editorial Freelancers Association and *Publishers Weekly*, respectively. Every two years, EFA surveys its membership on the subject of professional practices, which includes rates, and then publishes the results.[1] These results are presented in the form of graphs that show the ranges of rates for particular types of work in specific areas, such as copyediting textbooks, writing brochures for

---

* This excellent article by Barbara Reitt, which gives detailed information on determining a business budget as a preliminary step to figuring day, hourly, and page rates, is well worth reading as a supplement to this chapter.

Table 1. *Hourly Rate Ranges among Skills and Editorial Settings (Figures from 1992)*

Settings	Copy-editing	Proof-reading	Editing	Rewriting	Writing	Indexing
Publishers						
Books	$ 9–121	$ 9–30	$12–100	$13–100	$10–75	$ 7–95
Magazines	13–25	10–31	15–35	25–50	15–55	25–50
Ann. rep.	18–40	14–40	15–20	–a	–	–
Catalogs	15–30	12–20	15–30	23–30	22–50	–
Ad copy	12–30	15–30	15–35	–	22–75	–
Other	12–28	10–22	15–125	15–125	4–125	–
Corporate						
Books	15–40	11–40	15–100	20–100	20–75	18–50
Magazines	15–40	14–40	15–55	30–35	4–75	–
Ann. rep.	15–75	14–40	15–50	–	–	–
Catalogs	18–40	15–40	18–30	20–22	22–50	22–50
Ad copy	12–50	12–35	12–40	12–50	22–200	–
Other	12–28	12–50	20–75	20–75	11–200	–
Nonprofit						
Books	9–27	9–26	13–40	18–40	20–40	–
Magazines	9–50	9–25	12–40	–	17–30	–
Ann. rep.	12–26	12–25	12–25	25–70	–	–
Catalogs	–	15–18	18–26	–	–	–
Ad copy	–	–	–	–	40–60	–
Other	14–35	5–15	14–50	14–50	10–60	–

Source: *Professional Practices Survey,* Editorial Freelancers Association, New York,
        March 1994.

a A dash is used when only one person responded, or when there was no response at all.

nonprofit organizations, or indexing trade nonfiction books. Table 1 is a summary of the results of the 1994 survey, but since the figures cited were current in 1992, they will be outdated by the time you read this. The table is provided solely to show how wide the spread of ranges is for the various editorial specialties, and not as a guide to what you should be charging for them.

A third way of finding out the "standard" or going rate is to call one of the freelance organizations listed in Appendix C2 and ask them what rates you should be charging. Or you could even call several publishers and ask what their rates are, although you should be prepared to be told that that information is confidential. Also, at least one house I work for has two sets of rates: one for straight copyediting and another for what they call "express editing" (more on this later), which requires you to turn 300 pages a week and therefore is slightly higher.

Publishing versus Business Clients

One of the things a freelancer is constantly hearing is that business clients pay better than mainstream publishers. The truth of this statement in incontestable, but not all sky is blue. By which I mean that "business" is not always the rich uncle we hear it is. For example, one of the ten top accounting firms in the country paid me only $6 an hour when I started freelancing for them in 1979. And in the mid-1980s, when a couple of well-known pharmaceutical houses listed copyediting jobs on the EFA Job Phone, the rate they offered was no more than what publishers were paying.

If we define business as all areas *outside* traditional publishing, our definition will still be too broad, since that would include, for example, the small print shop on the third floor of a loft building that wants to pay $3 to $5 an hour for proofreading. Rather we tend to think of large corporations and most of their younger brothers and cousins: foundations, consulting firms, brokerage houses, law firms, advertising agencies, charities, and nonprofit organizations, to name a few.

Yet my first job in publishing was for a nonprofit company, an engineering society. Later, when I freelanced for them, they paid me about $7 an hour. Even though I should have been enlightened by this experience, the first glimmer didn't appear until a woman in a tailored business suit stood up at an EFA meeting and wondered aloud why, if members were having such difficulty living on the $8 or $9 an hour then being paid for copyediting, more of them didn't seek clients in industry, where they would be paid at least $20 an hour. To most of us this figure seemed as fanciful as Oz and about as attainable as the Holy Grail. Even so, everyone wanted to know more. I even wrote some letters to various corporations, but there was no response—probably because I was unaware of how difficult it is to pinpoint the person within a corporation to whom you need to talk if you're seeking editorial work (see Chapter 5 for more on this subject).

It might encourage you to know that many freelancers do manage to find their way into these higher paying assignments. But be warned. In 1981 I was recommended to what was described as a management consultant firm. Needless to say, I went to the interview with dollar signs in my heart. As it turned out, the lady doing the hiring had had no idea what rate to offer, so she'd called McGraw-Hill to find out what they paid their proofreaders and they had told her $8 an hour.

During my two decades of freelancing my clientele has included some corporate clients. I once worked briefly on a magazine that ITT was starting up. I had my own drawing account and was paid an excellent rate for the time (more on that negotiation in the next section). But for the most part my clients have either been professonal associations, textbook houses, or publishers of professional and reference books, with the occasional trade nonfiction house.

NEGOTIATING RATES

The biggest problem freelancers face vis-à-vis rates is being able to rise above ego (fear of rejection or a need to prove oneself) when establishing them.[4] In fact, "many a freelance exudes confidence when it comes to deciding which sentences need repair, . . . but turns apologetic and evasive when asked what these professional services will cost."[4] Also, when negotiating rates with higher paying clients, freelancers often miss out because they don't know what to ask for. For example, one of the most nerve-racking experiences of my freelance career occurred during my interview with the editor of the now defunct *ITT Programming*. I knew that if I handled things correctly, I stood a good chance of getting some of those big bucks we had been hearing so much about. Since I didn't know at what level to start the negotiations, my only (faint) hope was that he would mention a figure first. I was in a cold sweat because I knew that if I bid too low, he wouldn't hire me because at such a low rate I couldn't be very good. But if I bid too high, I risked pricing myself out of the job. As I write this, however, I see little cause for anxiety on this last count, since it's good negotiating practice to start high, thus leaving yourself some bargaining room. Still, at the time the situation felt like, if not exactly a Catch-22, at least a hangman's knot.

As it turned out, I couldn't maneuver him into stating a rate, so I finally had to screw up my courage and take a chance. I mentioned $20 per hour. He said that was acceptable, so naturally I became convinced that I could have gotten more if I'd asked for it. Such is the paranoia of the freelancer!

"Introductory" Rates

When most freelancers are just starting out, they tend to be overly accommodating. Hungry for those first jobs so they can start building a reputation and a client list, not to mention earning a living, they are willing to agree to whatever conditions the client offers. While such rationalizations may sound like a good idea on the surface, they tend to be more harmful than helpful. One of the worst rationalizations is the so-called "introductory" rate. Let me state it simply and succinctly: There is no such thing as an "introductory" rate. The reasons will become clear in the next section.

Bidding Low

"In general, the high earners [those who made more than $35,000] seemed to have a more businesslike attitude. No high earners said they would work cheaply just because they liked the subject matter, whereas five low earners [those who made less than $19,000] were always willing to work for less than usual if the subject appealed. A nice client is never an incentive to lower rates, according to six high earners and three low earners. Eleven low earners but only four high earners said they would always take a low-paying assignment if they needed money."[2]

While the numbers quoted have changed since this was published, the principles haven't. Thus we see that it's not just beginners who fall into the trap of bidding low in order to get a particular job. In some circumstances (see quote) seasoned freelancers are also tempted to bid or accept a low rate for a job. Most often the idea is that once the client has seen how good the editor is, the editor will be able to ask for (and get) a more desirable rate.

Should the client balk, the old freelancer paranoia kicks in: "If I stick to my guns, he'll just find some other hungry freelancer who'll be very happy to work for the money." Or the freelancer feels somehow obligated to the client and doesn't want to let him or her down. For whatever reason, the freelancer is stuck in the trap. And after a while, people who are willing to work for less tend to think less of themselves and their abilities. Since in reality it is almost impossible to negotiate up—at least for six months to a year, when it would be normal to ask for a raise—it is better to insist on at least the current going publishing rate in the beginning. While it may lose you a couple of jobs, sometimes what at first looks like a mistake, will end up working in your favor.

A case in point. Sometime during the middle of the summer of 1980, about three years after I'd started freelancing, I got a call from Marilyn Salmansohn, whom I'd worked with at the IEEE. She was now Managing Editor at the Association for Computing Machinery. Would I be interested in working on one of their publications?

I arrived at the interview with a fresh copy of my résumé, which I handed to her as I sat down. We chatted awhile, and she told me about what the job entailed. Did it sound like something I'd like to do? Outwardly calm, I answered yes. The rest of the interview went something like this:

"I notice on your résumé that your rate is ten dollars. I'm afraid I can only offer six. Would that be okay with you?"

It would not, though I was tempted to say yes out of friendship.

"Well, what if we say six-fifty, with a raise to seven in, say, three months?"

This sounded possible, but I said, "I couldn't do it for less than eight."

The interview ended shortly afterward, both of us sorry we couldn't reach an agreement but both unwilling or unable to negotiate further. As I walked home, I tried to find some reason to accept the lower offer and almost had myself convinced by the time I arrived back at my apartment. In the end, however, I listened to my insides and to my wife, and regretfully let the opportunity pass.

A few weeks later Marilyn called and asked if I was still willing to take the job at $8. During the interval she had somehow managed to convince her bosses that it was worth spending a couple of extra dollars to get someone who knew what he was doing. Not all such cases turn out as happily as this one, but you have to be willing to take the risk. If I hadn't, I would have been working for less money than I was comfortable with and been miserable into the bargain.

Another difficulty with taking low-paying jobs is that doing so can be an unnecessary drain on your self-esteem. On the other hand, in many circumstances it's a plus to have a part-time job when you're freelancing, because then you have a source of steady rather than fluctuating income. A case in point is a colleague who had two such jobs, one of which was as a clerk in a bookstore. Although this work provided her with a steady income, it didn't cover all her expenses—but without it she would have had no income to carry her while she sought freelance jobs in her field.

In spite of the preceding discussion, however, there are ways that you can professionally justify taking a low-paying job. For example, when you balance it with work from higher paying clients, or when the client agrees to compensate you for some expense that the job entails, such as by providing a special kind of software required by the project.[4]

SPECIAL RATES

There are occasions when you should ask for more than the going rate. For example, when I started freelancing, everyone told me that because I was a technical copyeditor and could work on math, engineering, and computer books, I would be able to command a higher rate than someone who worked on less demanding manuscripts. In the event, this has never proved to be the case, for the simple reason that my skills aren't specialized enough.

What do I mean by specialized skills, or knowledge? Let's suppose you have been fascinated with eighteenth-century ordnance since reading your first Horatio Hornblower adventure as a high school sophomore. Over the ensuing years you've made an exhaustive study of the subject and have several standard reference works on it in your personal library. One day you get a call from a publisher that needs someone to copyedit a book on the weaponry of the American War for Independence. Since there probably aren't many people with that sort of arcana at their fingertips, the fact that you have this special knowledge should enable you to get a few extra dollars an hour.

Other occasions when you would be justified in asking for a higher rate are when your client wants you to do heavy editing (which can include rewriting and reorganizing; see Chapter 1), and when the schedule is tight.

As I said earlier, I have a client that has a category called "express editing." By this they mean that they expect me to turn 300 pages a week instead of the usual one to two hundred. Even though these manuscripts are generally pretty clean or are tear sheet copy,* and therefore require only a light copyedit, I still need to free up a block of time in order to do them. For this reason and because of the smaller time frame, the company pays, say, $17 per hour rather than their usual $15.

INCREASING YOUR RATE

There are essentially three ways of increasing your rate, and two of them involve asking. The most prevalent is illustrated by the following story. At a meeting of the now defunct EFA Affinity Group on Trade Nonfiction one of the panelists said that when she asked her assistant in charge of freelancers if any of them were ever given increases, the answer was, "Yes, but they have to ask for it." As I say, this is the usual practice, so when you feel you're due for a raise, ask your in-house contact. You needn't be bashful about it. After all, most of the people you are working for will be sympathetic, many having freelanced themselves at some time in their careers.

While we're on the subject of raises, let's look at the exception to the "you have to ask for it" rule. Although it's true that most places will continue to pay you the same rate until you ask for a raise, a few copy chiefs automatically give their freelancers periodic raises, even though it may not amount to more than a dollar or two an hour. According to an article in the *EFA Newsletter* "clients may actually recognize when skilled freelancers are charging too little. Eight (40%) of the 20 free-

---

* Tear sheets are pages torn from the previous edition and pasted on a blank piece of paper. Sometimes art is also submitted this way, even though it's not always usable in this format.

lancers who earned between $15,000 and $20,000 received unsolicited raises in 1990. By comparison, the Rates Survey reported that 28% of respondents overall were given unsolicited raises."[5]

The third way of getting a raise is to find clients that are willing to pay your new rate. I know this sounds simplistic, but it's not always that easy to do. Let's say you're making $15 an hour, but think your work is worth $5 more than that. The next time a client calls, tell her your new rate is $20. She'll either say okay, or she'll have to check and get back to you. If (or when) she says no, you can either try and negotiate an intermediate amount, or you can say no. It's worth noting again that freelancing is a business and freelancers should be willing to say *no* when the situation warrants. One woman who uses this method says you have to be willing to lose some clients (at least for a while), but that eventually you'll find yourself working at the rate you consider justified. And it wouldn't hurt to approach new sources as well, citing your new rate, of course.

The least desirable way to get a higher rate than was contracted for is bill padding. Although unethical, this practice is encouraged by low hourly rates as well as by in-house editors who are sympathetic to the freelancer's situation. In some instances, however, the practice can work against the freelancer, as when a client is lost because the padding is too obvious. This can also result in a diminution of the freelancer's professional reputation. Therefore, rather than padding or agreeing to pad, a freelancer could ask what the budget for the project is and then say something like, "What I propose doing is charging my regular rate of $25 an hour, and I'll stay within the budget. If I find there's a problem after I've worked a few hours, I'll call and we can renegotiate." This way freelancers maintain their integrity while at the same time satisfying their clients.[6]

Since most freelancers are resourceful and creative people, you might be able to find other ways to increase your rate. I once published my résumé in a book of sample résumés. In it, I gave my rate as $20 per hour, which was the increase I wanted. The next person who called with a job had seen my listing, and was prepared to pay me that amount. It's sometimes a slow process, but eventually your new rate will prevail.

Now that we've investigated rates and how to determine them, it's time to talk about their practical application. We do this in the next chapter, which is on billing.

NOTES

1. *Professional Practices Survey,* Editorial Freelancers Association, New York, March 1994.
2. Laurie Lewis, "Work Styles of the Rich and Famished," *EFA Newsletter,* vol. XVI, no. 2, November-December 1991, p. 3.
3. Sylvia Nasar, "Statistics Reveal Bulk of New Jobs Pay Over Average," *The New York Times,* October 17, 1994, p. A1.
4. Barbara B. Reitt, "Setting Fees Rationally," *Scholarly Publishing,* vol. 22, no. 3 (University of Toronto Press, Toronto, Ontario, Canada), April 1991, pp. 166, 155, and 168.
5. Laurie Lewis, "Hourly Rates of Top-Earning and Low-Income Freelancers," *EFA Newsletter,* vol. XVI, no. 4, April-May 1992, p. 4.
6. "Padding Bills Against Low Rates? Not a Fair Practice, No Matter Whose Suggestion," *Freelance Editorial Association News,* vol. 8, no. 2, Spring/Summer 1992, p. 2.

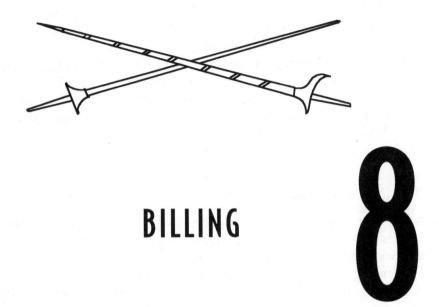

BILLING

8

Recently I overheard a young man on the street telling his companions that he had psychologically fallen back into his "impoverished artist routine" of just getting by from month to month. This is a familiar state (and state of mind) to many editorial freelancers, and it isn't an easy one to overcome, short of winning the lottery. Even so, that windfall would likely have the same effect on many people that extra money has on the mother in D. H. Lawrence's "The Rocking Horse Winner"—that is, it would be seen not as a means of paying off current debt and planning sensibly for the future, but as a license to spend more.

Therefore, just as asking for a certain rate or for a raise can be a problem for many editorial freelancers, so, in some circumstances, can billing for *all* of the hours they work. For example, suppose you accept a job and agree, without close scrutiny, that you can accomplish it within a certain time frame, say ten pages an hour for a total of fifty hours. Once you get into it, however, you discover that some of the processes (e.g., rewriting certain chapters) are taking you longer than you anticipated. You want to do a good job, but have been told that the budget won't allow any leeway in terms of the number of hours spent on the job. Here, clearly, is a situation where you should call your client and discuss your concerns and hope for a renegotiation, but many freelancers find this prospect daunting when they have already said "can do." Thus, the only apparent solution is to absorb the cost of the extra time and hope to make it back on future, less complex projects where a couple of extra hours can be added into each bill.

But these and similarly worrisome situations aside, billing involves more than just filling out a form and sending it in. Timing your invoices so you create a useful cash flow is also crucial. In the following sections we discuss cash flow along with the more routine aspects of making out a bill. We also explain some ways of dealing with clients who take too long to pay.

BILLING STRATEGIES

Let's start with a story—one might say a horror story, though not of the H. P. Lovecraft and Bram Stoker type. Rather, this is a tale of one editorial freelancer's billing odyssey.

Although the assignment started out well, Dan came to consider it cursed. Things began normally enough with the offer of an editing job by a company for which he had already done some proofreading. He was also told that he had "plenty of leeway." He therefore attacked the text with gusto, as any editor would when faced with a poorly prepared manuscript. The client, however, failed to mention one small item: the budget for the project. All seemed to be going well until after Dan submitted his bill. Then he was informed that he had exceeded the editing budget by 100 percent and that the publisher wanted documentary proof of all his hours. Fortunately, he'd kept his time sheets (see Chapter 6), so he was able to comply with the request. Still, it was four months before he received his money. As further evidence of the "curse," he later found out that after he had done the work, one of the authors had fallen ill, as had the project editor, and that the authors and the publisher had squabbled, all of which had resulted in cancellation of the project.

This story illustrates, among other things, the importance of keeping complete and accurate records of the time you spend working on a project. Other aspects of billing covered in this section are billable expenses, bill forms, and cash flow.

Charting Expenses

In Chapter 6 we saw how a time sheet might be kept. Now we have seen one reason why it should be kept. Another, more obvious reason is that when it comes time to prepare your bill you need to know how many hours to charge for. But time spent marking copy isn't the only billable expense you'll incur during the course of a project. Among the other expenses are the following:

Time spent traveling to and from a client's office. This means portal-to-portal time, just as your plumber charges you when he or she comes to fix a leaky pipe. I have found that I can reach most of my clients within a half-hour, either by bus or by subway, so I just add in an extra hour for each trip, plus any time spent on their premises (see immediately below). I also record this separately in my diary; viz., "Went up to Z-Prop to drop off ms. Was there 1¼ hours, including one hour travel time."

Time spent at a client's office. This includes the total amount of time you spend there, even if some of it is spent talking about non-business-related subjects. I figure if my clients want to tell me about their vacation or how their children behave in preschool, that's their decision. It's not that I don't enjoy hearing about these things—I do—but as a professional person, my time is also worth something.

Time spent talking on the telephone with your editor or other company employee and/or the author, or if you need to conduct phone interviews. If I have to talk with someone about some aspect of a project, I often call them as a break in the work. Making the call this way is easier from the standpoint of recordkeeping; I just leave the clock running. If it's long-distance, I record the time of the call and the area code in my diary, otherwise I'll never remember it when I get my phone bill. Again, you can charge for the entire call, as long as a portion of it was business-related.

Any supplies or equipment you needed to buy specifically for that project. This sort of charge is unusual, since even the cost of a special dictionary can be taken as a tax deduction as an addition to your reference library. But there are occasions when you may want to recover some costs from the client—such as the cost of a particular type of calculator or specially printed letterhead stationery. If you decide to go this route, and your client agrees to reimburse you for these expenses and does so separately from your fee, you can take them later on your taxes as business deductions. By the same token, if your client reimburses these costs along with the fee (as most of them will), so that together they appear as income on the 1099 (the freelancer's W-2; for more on 1099s, see Chapter 9), you can claim them as business expenses.

Any other project-related travel. I once copyedited a financial-advice book for teenagers written by Sylvia Porter (*Your Own Money*, Avon, 1983)—I even got them to put my name on the copyright page as the copyeditor (see Chapter 6). At the beginning of the editing process, my immediate boss was sent to Florida to discuss editing-related questions and concerns with Ms. Porter. Suppose, however, that the editor had become ill and the company had decided to send me in her place. In that case, any job-related expenses I incurred, such as taxi fares to and from Ms. Porter's home, or any supplies, such as cassettes for my tape recorder, could be charged back to the company. If you ever find yourself in this or a similar situation, remember to get receipts for all these expenses.

Any mailing or messenger costs, including overnight mail services. There are rare occasions when an editorial freelancer will hire a messenger, but the more usual practice is for the client to have its regular messenger service make any pickups and deliveries. On the question of whether or not you should tip the messenger, the answer is no. Living in New York, where everyone expects a tip, and knowing how little these people are paid, I always feel awkward about not tipping, but on the few occasions I've tried to, the messenger has refused the offer.

Overnight mail services would include Express Mail, Federal Express, UPS, *et alia.* Many publishing companies, however, have charge accounts with these services and will give you the account number to save you the out-of-pocket expense and themselves the trouble of reimbursing you. If they tell you to use one of these services, but don't mention an account number, ask if they have one. It could save you some trouble; for instance, if you want to use one of the service's special collection boxes. If you do decide to send the package from the local office of an overnight mail service, however, your travel and waiting time are billable expenses.

Fax and photocopying costs. Most of these costs are so minimal that I don't charge them back to the client but simply take them as deductions on my taxes. I also record them in my diary as I incur them. I do have one client, however, who insists that I photocopy all manuscript pages I send in because their overnight mail service, while inexpensive, is unreliable. In other words, packages have been lost with enough frequency to justify this extra precaution. Since a batch might cost anywhere between $20 and $50 to photocopy—cash, not plastic (sometimes a major consideration)—I always include the cost on my invoice. When you add these expenses to your bill, remember to attach receipts and to keep copies in the project file (see Chapter 6).

Meals or other project-related entertainment expenses. In the majority of cases, editorial freelancers never meet their authors, let alone entertain them in restaurants, cocktail lounges, private clubs, or their own homes. And while they may have lunch or dinner with a client, such costs are usually taken as business-related tax deductions (see Chapters

6 and 9 for details). This item, however, may become an issue for writers, especially should they use such social occasions for preliminary
meetings with individuals they plan to interview, or for the interview
itself.

Any other expense that is specifically related to the project in question.

Although the items just listed are all legitimate, recoverable expenses, many of them are absorbed by freelancers and later taken as tax
deductions. For example, most freelancers won't bother to charge back
the cost of a floppy disk or phone calls (except, of course, for the time
involved). In the case of the disk, the cost is so minimal that it can be
recovered nonspecifically by adding in an extra quarter-hour; in the
case of long distance phone calls, even though you charge the client for
them, you can still include them as part of your telephone deduction
on your taxes. Also, although many of your clients have lines on their
bill forms for photocopying, mailing, and telephone expenses, many
more don't, for the simple reason that itemized expenses make things
more complicated for their accounting department. Therefore they'd
much rather you recover such costs through billable time. If you're
billing the client for certain expenses, like overnight mail services or
photocopying, you must attach receipts to your bill. In these cases, I
always keep a copy of the receipt in the folder for that project (see
Chapter 6). Just about the only cost that I routinely recover is for
overnight mail services—the rest, which are usually minimal, I take as
business deductions.

The Bill Form

Now that you've tallied all your billable expenses, you need a vehi-
cle for conveying them to your client: the bill form. Bill forms are of two
main types, the client's and your own (for a sample of the latter, see
Figure 1). Most of my clients, which include major textbook, professional and reference book, and trade nonfiction publishers, provide
their own bill form, and all I have to do is fill in the blanks. If none is
included with the manuscript when the job is sent to you, check with
your client to see if this was an oversight or if you should use your own
form. Whichever one you use for a particular project, you should
include the following information:

1. Your name and address.
2. The name and address of the client. Unless told oth-
    erwise, you can address your bill to the person
    you're working for.

```
INVOICE

Vendor # 156825


TO:  Edith Editor
Preppy Publishers, Ltd.
6060 Fifth Avenue
New York, NY 10000



FROM:  Frieda Freelancer
660 West 22nd Street
New York, NY 10011


FOR:  Copyediting Chapters 1 - 9, Frontmatter, Glossary,
Selected Readings, and Appendixes A - E (266 pages), 118
figures,and 7 pages of figure legends for Mett/Sheff, Food
for the Nineties:  New Strategies for Home Cookery and
Restaurant Cuisine


PERIOD COVERED:  11/15/94 - 11/29/94


TOTAL HOURS:   26 1/2 @ $16/hr


TOTAL BILL:  $447.75 (includes $23.75 for Express Mail)



Signed:_____

Date:_____
Social Security Number:  000-00-0000
```

Figure 1. Sample bill form.

3. The title and author of the book you worked on.
   Some publishers also want the ISBN number, but
   this is usually added in-house.
4. What work was accomplished; i.e., copyediting,
   proofreading, etc.
5. Number of pages, number of illustrations, number
   of captions or number of pages of captions, and
   number of tables.
6. Number of hours worked.
7. Rate per hour.
8. Other billable expenses, such as photocopying and
   overnight mail services.
9. Total amount of bill.
10. Your Social Security number and, if applicable, your
    vendor number.
11. Your signature.
12. The date.
13. Some clients will want to know whether this is a
    partial or final bill. Partial bills are covered in the
    Cash Flow section below.
14. Many clients will want the inclusive dates covering
    the period you worked on the project.

Most of these items are self-evident and, when you think about them, obvious. However, not all of your clients will require all of this information. For some, the title of the project; the name of the author; the number of articles (for magazines and journals) or pages (for books) edited, or number of galleys proofread; the number of hours worked; the hourly rate; and the total amount will suffice. If you're seeking reimbursement for some expenses, remember to attach receipts.

When you've finished making out your bill, enter the pertinent details in your work log (see Figure 2 in Chapter 6) and make a copy of the bill form for the file.

While the bill form may seem routine and innocuous, it must be filled out correctly and completely or you will experience delays in getting paid. Usually your client will review your bill before passing it on to his or her superior or to the accounting department. If errors or omissions are found, they will call right away to correct them. For example, I once had a call from an in-house editor telling me I'd made an arithmetic error and wanting to know which was correct, the number of hours worked or the total amount of the bill. If the hours were correct, the total amount needed to be changed; if the total amount was right, the number of hours was wrong. We corrected the error, but if she hadn't found it or taken the time to call me, I might not have been paid on time.

If clients do not catch such errors, the result will be a call from the accounting department several weeks later asking for your Social Security number or informing you of an error in your arithemtic. In some cases this can result in payment being delayed for another two to four weeks, depending on the length of that company's check-writing cycle.

Cash Flow

One difficulty I have with taking more than a week off for vacation is reestablishing a viable cash flow once I get back. This can take from four to six months, the reason being the "dead" time caused by first getting and doing the work and then waiting to be paid for it. One project can therefore account for two months, depending on the size of the job and the time it takes the client to pay.

One freelancer I know has developed a partial solution to this problem. Before going on vacation, he sends postcards to all his clients announcing the dates he'll be away and closing with the suggestion that, upon his return, he'll be available to work on new projects. While this may assure him work when he gets back from sunnier climes, it doesn't entirely solve the time-lapse problem.

For most editorial freelancers, cash flow is therefore a crucial issue, especially when they haven't much leeway between expenses and income. For example, I know a freelancer who returned from two weeks vacation to find over $3000 waiting for him. Even so, he had to rely mainly on credit lines and other resources to get him through the next three months. This not only depleted his reserves, but also increased his debt load, making it even more difficult to make ends meet.

I tell this story to illustrate the importance of cash flow, not to warn you off vacations.

Cash flow can be defined as timing your bills so that you have sufficient money coming in to cover expenses at the times you need it. Such a flow cannot be established by the proceeds of just one job. While that job may cover expenses two or four weeks hence, what about the two or four weeks after that, or some other period in between? That will take more work. Thus a freelancer might have to complete or partially complete up to six or eight assignments before a viable cash flow is established. Of course, you also need a steady and reliable supply of work, or the cash flow will rapidly dwindle to a trickle. While some people thrive on this sort of uncertainty—they see it as a challenge to be met and overcome—others find that the uncertainty causes too much wear and tear on their nerves and decide to seek an in-house job with a regular paycheck.

The objective for the freelancer thus is to accomplish enough work during the "fat" periods to establish sufficient reserves to carry him or her through leaner times. (Remember, the editorial process is often cyclical, especially in textbook editing, with periods of copyediting followed by periods of proofreading.) This is the major reason why it is best to be able to do a variety of tasks (copyediting, proofreading, indexing, research, etc.) and to have more than one client.

Partial Billing

A crucial element in establishing cash flow is partial billing. Partial billing is exactly what it sounds like: submitting bills for different sections of a copyediting or proofreading project as they are completed. For example, you might be offered a textbook of over 1000 manuscript pages and several hundred tables and illustrations. The job might be scheduled to last two or three months, which is a long time for a freelancer to work without getting paid. The client will also want the edited manuscript back in batches so the author can start checking the editing and the corrected pages can start flowing to the compositor. The client will therefore suggest that the freelancer include an invoice with each batch of manuscript. In this way, the freelancer receives checks at three two- to four-week intervals, depending on how fast the client pays its bills. On the down side, although it's been a long time since it's happened to me, I have known accounting departments to foil these intentions by collecting the partial bills and paying them all at the end of the project—in order to write fewer checks.

As I just indicated, partial billing is only possible during long-term projects, or manuscripts of 600 or more pages. Since, depending on the complexity of the project, most publishers expect a freelance copyeditor to turn between 100 and 200 pages a week, it's only fair that they allow the freelancer to bill in installments. Although partial billing is fairly standard practice on these longer projects, it is still a good idea to ask if it's all right to bill with each batch. Often the client will tell you to bill this way while explaining the project to you, but if they don't, it's okay to ask. The rule-of-thumb is to break the project into three batches, and to bill with each batch.

Depending on the length of the job, you can also do partial billing on any project where you're receiving a flat fee. For example, on some projects, such as textbook development and rewriting, the work can last from nine months to a year and a half, and can bring in between $6000 and $12,000 or more over that period. In these cases, some publishers want monthly invoices showing the number of hours worked that month; others allow billing in three or four installments for a third or a quarter of the flat fee.

To summarize, with long-term editing projects (e.g., manuscripts of 600 pages or more) where the client wants the edited work returned in batches of approximately equal length, you should be able to bill with each batch, thus creating a mini-cash-flow of three checks staggered two to four weeks apart, depending on your client's turnaround time.

SLOW PAYERS

Sometimes you'll run across a company, usually a small one, that takes more than a month to pay. This tardiness may be due to cash flow problems, or the company may be teetering on the verge of bankruptcy; a variety of other causes are also possible. But regardless of the reason, how does an editorial freelancer deal with the situation? The most often recommended way is to follow these four steps:

1. The first thing you should do when a client is late in paying your bill is call the person you were working for to let them know there's a problem and ask them to check on it for you. Usually that person is unaware of the situation and will be happy to follow through. You may have to make three or four such calls, spaced a few days apart, before you can be sure nothing is being done. One sign could be a change in your contact's attitude toward you or evidence that he or she is avoiding your calls.

2. Once you realize that the in-house editor is unable to accomplish anything for you, you should write a letter to that person's supervisor explaining the problem and requesting payment, with copies to the company president and the comptroller. You should be able to get their names either from your in-house contact or from the receptionist. In the letter you should clearly state your case (without hysteria and threats) and request payment. You could also include a comment about industry standards for the timing of payments. To do this, consult a copy of the *Professional Practices Survey* published by the Editorial Freelancers Association to see how long it took the repondents' slowest paying clients to pay.[1] In the 1992 survey, you would see that only 53 of the 308 respondents, or 17.2 percent, reported clients that took longer than one month to pay them. On the other hand, 107, or 34.7 percent, reported clients that took one month to pay.[1] Knowing this, you could cite the latter figure in your letter; that is, you might say that "34.7 percent

(the majority) of members' clients pay within four weeks." (On this subject, it might be encouraging for you to know that of the 309 members who responded to the question, only 30 [or 9.7 percent] reported being stiffed by a client.[1])

3. If this letter doesn't work, you should try to find a lawyer who will write a letter to the company on his or her letterhead, stating your case and requesting immediate payment. Lawyers are generally expensive, and such a letter could cost up to $500. But don't despair. You can probably find a lawyer who will do this for you as part of his or her pro bono work. One way to locate such a lawyer is to see if your area has an organization similar to New York City's Volunteer Lawyers for the Arts, through which you can find a lawyer who will write the letter either pro bono or for a much reduced fee. Otherwise, check with friends and relatives to see if they know a lawyer who could help you for a modeate fee. Another option, at least in New York City, is to call the Legal Referral Service of the Association of the Bar of the City of New York (see Appendix C3 under Miscellaneous Services) (other local bar associations may have similar services; check your phone book for more information). This service will provide you with the name of a qualified lawyer. Your call to the lawyer is free, and you would use it to set up an appointment for a half-hour interview that would cost $25. The fee for any work actually done by the lawyer would be negotiated. The Referral Service has no information on lawyers who might do the work on a pro bono basis; the best place to find such a lawyer is through Volunteer Lawyers for the Arts, or, if you live outside the New York City area, a similar volunteer lawyers group in your community (for more information on these, see Appendix C3 under Miscellaneous Services and the Bibliography). Why go through this process? Because many companies want to avoid legal entanglements, and the sight of a lawyer's letterhead will probably be enough to pry your money out of them.

4. If a lawyer's letter fails to help, you still have a last resort—take 'em to court! I don't recommend that you go this route if you want to work for the client again—but after this experience, why would you? Many states have something called Small Claims Court as part of their judicial setup. This is an informal court for people who want to recover sums of money totaling not more than $3000, without using a lawyer.[2] Of course your area may not have a small claims court, but a regular subpoena could have the same effect. For most companies, receipt of the notice will be enough to bring forth your money—if your client can't afford to pay you, they certainly can't afford attorney's fees and probable court costs. One argument against this assumption is that

many companies have lawyers on retainer, but in such cases going to court and explaining why they haven't paid your bill isn't worth the hassle.

If you go to Small Claims Court, your initial costs, which are recoverable from your client only if you win the case, are the filing fee and the cost of mailing the notice to your client (about $5.00).[2] If you want to learn more about the process, New York State publishes a free booklet titled *A Guide to Small Claims Court* that you can get by calling the State of New York Office of Court Administration. Other guides to the subject are *Small Claims Guide for Town and Village Courts,* by Herbert Kline et al., and *How to Get Your Day (Or Night) in Small Claims Court,* by Eric A. Goldstein.

Also, some advocacy groups, such as the Freelance Editorial Association in Boston, offer their members a service that talks a person through the steps necessary to recover fees from late payers. Otherwise, there are two additional ways of dealing with late payers: barter and late fees.

A number of years ago a colleague and I both did freelance work for a computer magazine that eventually went into Chapter 11 bankruptcy. We both went on accepting work from the company much too long, but we liked the person we were working for and the money—when we managed to collect it—was good. At first they were slow in paying, and then the checks started bouncing. After we (and other vendors) complained enough, they began paying with cashier's checks. Once, after a check had been returned, my client paid me out of her own pocket; that's when I discovered that the company was bouncing its employees' checks as well! In the end I got all the monies owed me before finally refusing to do any more work for them. Earlier in the game, however, my colleague worked out a barter deal with the client whereby she was paid in software instead of cash. Since the magazine published reviews of new computer software and hardware, they had lots of copies of reviewed software lying around. I believe my friend earned copies of two programs she needed before she severed relations with the company. Thus, in some circumstances barter can work to the advantage of both parties.

Late fees were mentioned earlier, in Chapter 6. As I said then, even though this is not yet an accepted practice in the publishing industry, it is practiced by most other businesses, small and large. What you do is put a line at the bottom of your standard bill form stating that bills paid after thirty days (or some other reasonable period) will be subject to a small surcharge, say 2 percent. If you haven't been paid in the stated time frame, resubmit your bill with the 2 percent charge clearly added in. As an added incentive to timely payment, you could likewise offer a 2 percent reduction on the amount owed if payment is made within, say, two weeks.

Now that we have reviewed the various billing procedures and ways of handling slow payers, we are ready to take a look at the last major issues confronting editorial freelancers— taxes, insurance, and retirement. The following chapter provides a basic guide to the various taxes editorial freelancers must pay, including a review of the different tax forms, and a brief look at some of the insurance and retirement plans available to independent contractors.

NOTES

1. *Editorial Freelancers Association Professional Practices Survey,* Editorial Freelancers Association, New York, 1994, p. 5.
2. *A Guide to Small Claims Court, New York State Unified Court System,* Judith S. Kaye and Matthew T. Crosson, New York, rev. April 1993, pp. 1 and 2.

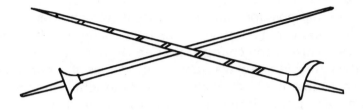

SOME FINANCIAL CONCERNS

9

Although editorial freelancers may not want to face them, three important financial concerns need to be addressed by anyone operating a freelance business: taxes, retirement plans, and insurance. The purpose of this chapter is to make readers aware of some of their obligations and options in these areas. I am not an expert in either tax preparation or financial planning, so I can't go into much depth on these subjects. There are, however, plenty of highly qualified professionals who can answer any questions that are not answered in this chapter.

Many freelancers aren't aware of all their tax obligations. The first section of this chapter therefore deals with the major business-related taxes for which editorial freelancers are responsible. But financial planning doesn't end with careful tax planning. Editorial freelancers need to be aware of some of the many retirement plans and insurance options available to them. Later sections of this chapter discuss those plans, but readers should consult experts in those fields for additional information and guidance.

TAXES

Taxes are often a mystery to editorial freelancers, who are not always aware of *all* the ones to which they are subject. Also, no matter how long you've been filling out your own forms, you still may not be taking all of the deductions to which you're entitled. Up until a few years ago, I was in that position, and then I discovered another one! In part, this may have occurred because the tax laws change so often that we're not always aware of the changes that apply to editorial freelancers. Finding the new deduction was just one in a series of events that led me to hire an accountant, something I'd always thought I couldn't afford to do. My new accountant immediately filed a couple of amended returns so I could get refunds for some past taxes I'd overpaid. In addition, he found some other ways to save me money, one being opening an IRA (more on these later in the chapter), something else I had long thought I couldn't afford. The truth is that freelancers cannot afford *not* to use a professional tax adviser and make some kind of provision for their later years, even if they don't plan to retire.

Since I am neither an accountant, nor a lawyer, nor any other kind of financial specialist, I am not an expert on taxes. This section therefore does not purport to explain the tax laws or to discuss the mechanics of filling out the many forms that freelancers must file. Instead, its purpose is to make the reader aware of the different forms that their *business* makes them responsible for filing. In other words, the discussion assumes that the reader is already familiar with the standard forms and schedules—1040, A, B, and so on—that any taxpayer must deal with at tax time. I also want to emphasize that, since the tax laws change so often, some of the information contained herein may no longer be current when you read the book. What we are concerned with in these two sections are brief descriptions of tax forms and IRS booklets.

Forms

Since freelancers often experience periods of low cash flow, many financial advisers suggest depositing 30 percent of each check received from a client into a special account (interest bearing, if possible). This way there should be sufficient funds to pay taxes when the tax bills come due.

The 1099. Since editorial freelancers are self-employed, they do not get a W-2 at tax time. Instead, each of their clients must send them a 1099 (Figure 1), on which the total amount of money received from that client is recorded. You should check this figure against your own records, since the totals won't always agree. The most common reason for this discrepancy is that the client may have included the amount of a bill you submitted in December, but which wasn't paid until January. Strictly speaking, this would be counted as income for the next tax year,

9595 ☐ VOID ☐ CORRECTED

PAYER'S name, street address, city, state, and ZIP code		1 Rents $ / 2 Royalties $ / 3 Other income $	OMB No. 1545-0115 **1994**	**Miscellaneous Income**
PAYER'S Federal identification number	RECIPIENT'S identification number	4 Federal income tax withheld $	5 Fishing boat proceeds $	**Copy A For Internal Revenue Service Center**
RECIPIENT'S name		6 Medical and health care payments $	7 Nonemployee compensation $	**File with Form 1096.**
Street address (including apt. no.)		8 Substitute payments in lieu of dividends or interest $	9 Payer made direct sales of $5,000 or more of consumer products to a buyer (recipient) for resale ▶ ☐	For Paperwork Reduction Act Notice and instructions for completing this form, see **Instructions for Forms 1099, 1098, 5498, and W-2G.**
City, state, and ZIP code		10 Crop insurance proceeds $	11 State income tax withheld $	
Account number (optional)	2nd TIN Not. ☐	12 State/Payer's state number		

Form **1099-MISC** Cat. No. 14425J Department of the Treasury - Internal Revenue Service

Figure 1. Form 1099.

not the current one. If a 1099 reports more income than your bills say you've received from a client, call and ask that they check their figures. If you're right, ask them to file an amended 1099 with the IRS.

A word of caution here: Employers are only required to file a 1099 if you've earned $600 or more from them during the tax year, but they may do so anyway. If they do, they are not required to send you a copy of the form. Therefore, freelancers are sometimes tempted not to include this "unreported" income. To avoid misunderstandings with the IRS at a later date, it is best to report *all* of your business income, regardless of whether you've received 1099s from all of your clients.

Your clients are required by the government to file their 1099s by the end of January. Therefore, if by the beginning of February you haven't received your copy from a client from which you've earned $600 or more during the past year, call to see if it has been sent.

Schedule C and Forms 8829 and 4562. Because editorial freelancers are sole proprietors, they must file Schedule C, Profit or Loss From Business (Figure 2). Since this is the form where you figure your net *business* income (or loss), including the business use of your car (Part IV), here is where all your recordkeeping pays off. Be aware, however, that this is not the form where you determine the expenses for the business use of your home. This is done on Form 8829 (Figure 3), which is also where you figure your home office deduction. This total is then entered on Schedule C. If you incur a capital expense for your business, such as the purchase of a computer or a new office chair, you can depreciate it over a specified period, usually five years. Or, if you prefer, you

SCHEDULE C
(Form 1040)

Department of the Treasury
Internal Revenue Service   (O)

Profit or Loss From Business
(Sole Proprietorship)

▶ Partnerships, joint ventures, etc., must file Form 1065.

▶ Attach to Form 1040 or Form 1041.   ▶ See Instructions for Schedule C (Form 1040).

OMB No. 1545-0074

1993

Attachment
Sequence No. 09

Name of proprietor

Social security number (SSN)

A   Principal business or profession, including product or service (see page C-1)

B   Enter principal business code
(see page C-6) ▶

C   Business name. If no separate business name, leave blank.

D   Employer ID number (EIN), if any

E   Business address (including suite or room no.) ▶
City, town or post office, state, and ZIP code

F   Accounting method: (1) ☐ Cash   (2) ☐ Accrual   (3) ☐ Other (specify) ▶

G   Method(s) used to   Lower of cost   Other (attach   Does not apply (if
value closing inventory: (1) ☐ Cost   (2) ☐ or market   (3) ☐ explanation)   (4) ☐ checked, skip line H)   Yes   No

H   Was there any change in determining quantities, costs, or valuations between opening and closing inventory? If "Yes," attach
explanation

I   Did you "materially participate" in the operation of this business during 1993? If "No," see page C-2 for limit on losses.

J   If you started or acquired this business during 1993, check here   ▶ ☐

Part I   Income

1	Gross receipts or sales. **Caution:** *If this income was reported to you on Form W-2 and the "Statutory employee" box on that form was checked, see page C-2 and check here* ▶ ☐	1
2	Returns and allowances	2
3	Subtract line 2 from line 1	3
4	Cost of goods sold (from line 40 on page 2)	4
5	**Gross profit.** Subtract line 4 from line 3	5
6	Other income, including Federal and state gasoline or fuel tax credit or refund (see page C-2)	6
7	**Gross income.** Add lines 5 and 6 ▶	7

Part II   Expenses. Caution: *Do not enter expenses for business use of your home on lines 8–27. Instead, see line 30.*

8	Advertising	8		19	Pension and profit-sharing plans	19
9	Bad debts from sales or services (see page C-3)	9		20	Rent or lease (see page C-4):	
10	Car and truck expenses (see page C-3)	10		a	Vehicles, machinery, and equipment	20a
11	Commissions and fees	11		b	Other business property	20b
12	Depletion	12		21	Repairs and maintenance	21
13	Depreciation and section 179 expense deduction (not included in Part III) (see page C-3)	13		22	Supplies (not included in Part III)	22
				23	Taxes and licenses	23
14	Employee benefit programs (other than on line 19)	14		24	Travel, meals, and entertainment:	
				a	Travel	24a
15	Insurance (other than health)	15		b	Meals and entertainment	
16	Interest:			c	Enter 20% of line 24b subject to limitations (see page C-4)	
a	Mortgage (paid to banks, etc.)	16a				
b	Other	16b		d	Subtract line 24c from line 24b	24d
17	Legal and professional services	17		25	Utilities	25
				26	Wages (less jobs credit)	26
18	Office expense	18		27	Other expenses (from line 46 on page 2)	27
28	Total expenses before expenses for business use of home. Add lines 8 through 27 in columns. ▶					28
29	Tentative profit (loss). Subtract line 28 from line 7					29
30	Expenses for business use of your home. Attach **Form 8829**					30

31   Net profit or (loss). Subtract line 30 from line 29.
• If a profit, enter on **Form 1040, line 12,** and ALSO on **Schedule SE, line 2** (statutory employees, see page C-5). Fiduciaries, enter on Form 1041, line 3.   } 31
• If a loss, you MUST go on to line 32.

32   If you have a loss, check the box that describes your investment in this activity (see page C-5).
• If you checked 32a, enter the loss on **Form 1040, line 12,** and ALSO on **Schedule SE, line 2** (statutory employees, see page C-5). Fiduciaries, enter on Form 1041, line 3.
• If you checked 32b, you MUST attach **Form 6198.**   }

32a ☐ All investment is at risk.
32b ☐ Some investment is not at risk.

For Paperwork Reduction Act Notice, see Form 1040 Instructions.   Cat. No. 11334P   Schedule C (Form 1040) 1993

Figure 2. Page 1 of Schedule C.

Form **8829**	**Expenses for Business Use of Your Home**	OMB No. 1545-1266
Department of the Treasury Internal Revenue Service (99)	▶ File only with Schedule C (Form 1040). Use a separate Form 8829 for each home you used for business during the year. ▶ See separate instructions.	**1994** Attachment Sequence No. **66**

Name(s) of proprietor(s)   Your social security number

Part I   Part of Your Home Used for Business

1	Area used regularly and exclusively for business, regularly for day care, or for inventory storage. See instructions	1	
2	Total area of home	2	
3	Divide line 1 by line 2. Enter the result as a percentage	3	%

• For day-care facilities not used exclusively for business, also complete lines 4–6.
• All others, skip lines 4–6 and enter the amount from line 3 on line 7.

4	Multiply days used for day care during year by hours used per day .	4	hr.
5	Total hours available for use during the year (365 days × 24 hours). See instructions	5	8,760 hr.
6	Divide line 4 by line 5. Enter the result as a decimal amount . . .	6	.
7	Business percentage. For day-care facilities not used exclusively for business, multiply line 6 by line 3 (enter the result as a percentage). All others, enter the amount from line 3 . . . . ▶	7	%

Part II   Figure Your Allowable Deduction

		(a) Direct expenses	(b) Indirect expenses	
8	Enter the amount from Schedule C, line 29, **plus** any net gain or (loss) derived from the business use of your home and shown on Schedule D or Form 4797. If more than one place of business, see instructions			8
	See instructions for columns (a) and (b) before completing lines 9–20.			
9	Casualty losses. See instructions	9		
10	Deductible mortgage interest. See instructions .	10		
11	Real estate taxes. See instructions	11		
12	Add lines 9, 10, and 11.	12		
13	Multiply line 12, column (b) by line 7 . . .		13	
14	Add line 12, column (a) and line 13.			14
15	Subtract line 14 from line 8. If zero or less, enter -0- .			15
16	Excess mortgage interest. See instructions . .	16		
17	Insurance	17		
18	Repairs and maintenance	18		
19	Utilities	19		
20	Other expenses. See instructions	20		
21	Add lines 16 through 20	21		
22	Multiply line 21, column (b) by line 7	22		
23	Carryover of operating expenses from 1993 Form 8829, line 41 . .	23		
24	Add line 21 in column (a), line 22, and line 23			24
25	Allowable operating expenses. Enter the smaller of line 15 or line 24			25
26	Limit on excess casualty losses and depreciation. Subtract line 25 from line 15			26
27	Excess casualty losses. See instructions	27		
28	Depreciation of your home from Part III below	28		
29	Carryover of excess casualty losses and depreciation from 1993 Form 8829, line 42	29		
30	Add lines 27 through 29			30
31	Allowable excess casualty losses and depreciation. Enter the smaller of line 26 or line 30 . .			31
32	Add lines 14, 25, and 31			32
33	Casualty loss portion, if any, from lines 14 and 31. Carry amount to Form 4684, Section B . .			33
34	Allowable expenses for business use of your home. Subtract line 33 from line 32. Enter here and on Schedule C, line 30. If your home was used for more than one business, see instructions ▶			34

Part III   Depreciation of Your Home

35	Enter the smaller of your home's adjusted basis or its fair market value. See instructions . .	35	
36	Value of land included on line 35	36	
37	Basis of building. Subtract line 36 from line 35	37	
38	Business basis of building. Multiply line 37 by line 7	38	
39	Depreciation percentage. See instructions	39	%
40	Depreciation allowable. Multiply line 38 by line 39. Enter here and on line 28 above. See instructions	40	

Part IV   Carryover of Unallowed Expenses to 1995

41	Operating expenses. Subtract line 25 from line 24. If less than zero, enter -0-	41	
42	Excess casualty losses and depreciation. Subtract line 31 from line 30. If less than zero, enter -0- .	42	

For Paperwork Reduction Act Notice, see page 1 of separate instructions.   Cat. No. 13232M   Form **8829** (1994)

8829:1

Figure 3. Page 1 of Form 8829.

can take it as a single deduction in the year of purchase. In either case, you must file Form 4562 (Figure 4).

Schedule SE. As mentioned earlier, editorial freelancers do not receive Form W-2. This is because, as self-employed people, they do not have an employer to withhold taxes and pay one-half of their Social Security and Medicare taxes. This means that editorial freelancers are responsible for the entire amount of these taxes.

The self-employment tax, currently about 18 percent, is one of the major business expenses an editorial freelancer will encounter. The correct form to use to figure this tax is Schedule SE, Self-Employment Tax (Figure 5). If you did not receive wages or tips, you can use Section A (Short Schedule SE). This tax is not entered on Schedule C as a business expense, but is entered directly onto Form 1040 as an additional tax. Be sure to read the instructions carefully, or you may miss the fact that you can enter a percentage of the total on Form 1040 (half in 1993) as an adjustment to income.

Form 1040-ES (OCR). Because their income varies from year to year, editorial freelancers are required to file the Estimated Tax for Individuals form, 1040-ES. Payments are made quarterly. After your initial filing, the IRS will send you the work sheet and payment vouchers at about the same time they send you your other tax forms. This is a separate mailing. If you do not receive them, you will need to pick them up at your local IRS office, or you can order them by calling 1-800-829-3676 (1-800-TAX-FORM). Also, if it looks as though your income will be radically different from your estimate, you may have to reestimate and file an amended declaration with your payment for the next quarter. In other words, if you realize in July that you are going to earn more (or less) money than you'd anticipated, depending on the amount of the increase (or decrease) you may have to file an amended return at the time you make your third payment in September. Read the instructions for details on filing amended estimates.

For New York City Residents

CAUTION: Even if you think these taxes do not apply to you, take note of them before going on to the next section so you can check your local tax requirements to see if you are subject to similar filings.

Editorial freelancers living in New York City who do their own taxes are not always aware of two taxes for which they are liable. These are the Unincorporated Business Tax (NYC-202 EZ), which is a 4 percent tax on net income from partnerships and sole proprietorships, and the

Form **4562**	**Depreciation and Amortization**	OMB No. 1545-0172
Department of the Treasury Internal Revenue Service (O)	**(Including Information on Listed Property)** ▶ See separate instructions. ▶ Attach this form to your return.	**1993** Attachment Sequence No. **67**

Name(s) shown on return | Identifying number

Business or activity to which this form relates

Part I   Election To Expense Certain Tangible Property (Section 179) (Note: *If you have any "Listed Property," complete Part V before you complete Part I.*)

1	Maximum dollar limitation (If an enterprise zone business, see instructions.)	**1**	$17,500
2	Total cost of section 179 property placed in service during the tax year (see instructions) . .	**2**	
3	Threshold cost of section 179 property before reduction in limitation	**3**	$200,000
4	Reduction in limitation. Subtract line 3 from line 2, but do not enter less than -0-	**4**	
5	Dollar limitation for tax year. Subtract line 4 from line 1, but do not enter less than -0-. (If married filing separately, see instructions.)	**5**	

	(a) Description of property	(b) Cost	(c) Elected cost	
6				

7	Listed property. Enter amount from line 26.	**7**	
8	Total elected cost of section 179 property. Add amounts in column (c), lines 6 and 7 . . .	**8**	
9	Tentative deduction. Enter the smaller of line 5 or line 8	**9**	
10	Carryover of disallowed deduction from 1992 (see instructions).	**10**	
11	Taxable income limitation. Enter the smaller of taxable income or line 5 (see instructions) . .	**11**	
12	Section 179 expense deduction. Add lines 9 and 10, but do not enter more than line 11 . .	**12**	
13	Carryover of disallowed deduction to 1994. Add lines 9 and 10, less line 12 ▶	**13**	

Note: *Do not use Part II or Part III below for listed property (automobiles, certain other vehicles, cellular telephones, certain computers, or property used for entertainment, recreation, or amusement). Instead, use Part V for listed property.*

Part II   MACRS Depreciation For Assets Placed in Service ONLY During Your 1993 Tax Year (Do Not Include Listed Property)

(a) Classification of property	(b) Month and year placed in service	(c) Basis for depreciation (business/investment use only—see instructions)	(d) Recovery period	(e) Convention	(f) Method	(g) Depreciation deduction
14 General Depreciation System (GDS) (see instructions):						
a 3-year property						
b 5-year property						
c 7-year property						
d 10-year property						
e 15-year property						
f 20-year property						
g Residential rental			27.5 yrs.	MM	S/L	
property			27.5 yrs.	MM	S/L	
h Nonresidential real				MM	S/L	
property				MM	S/L	
15 Alternative Depreciation System (ADS) (see instructions):						
a Class life					S/L	
b 12-year			12 yrs.		S/L	
c 40-year			40 yrs.	MM	S/L	

Part III   Other Depreciation (Do Not Include Listed Property)

16	GDS and ADS deductions for assets placed in service in tax years beginning before 1993 (see instructions)	**16**	
17	Property subject to section 168(f)(1) election (see instructions)	**17**	
18	ACRS and other depreciation (see instructions)	**18**	

Part IV   Summary

19	Listed property. Enter amount from line 25.	**19**	
20	Total. Add deductions on line 12, lines 14 and 15 in column (g), and lines 16 through 19. Enter here and on the appropriate lines of your return. (Partnerships and S corporations—see instructions)	**20**	
21	For assets shown above and placed in service during the current year, enter the portion of the basis attributable to section 263A costs (see instructions)	**21**	

For Paperwork Reduction Act Notice, see page 1 of the separate instructions.   Cat. No. 12906N   Form **4562** (1993)

Figure 4. Page 1 of Form 4562.

SCHEDULE SE
(Form 1040)

Department of the Treasury
Internal Revenue Service   (O)

Self-Employment Tax

► **See Instructions for Schedule SE (Form 1040).**

► **Attach to Form 1040.**

OMB No. 1545-0074

19**93**

Attachment
Sequence No. **17**

Name of person with **self-employment** income (as shown on Form 1040)

Social security number of person
with **self-employment** income ►

Who Must File Schedule SE

You must file Schedule SE if:

- Your wages (and tips) subject to social security AND Medicare tax (or railroad retirement tax) were less than $135,000; **AND**
- Your net earnings from self-employment from other than church employee income (line 4 of Short Schedule SE or line 4c of Long Schedule SE) were $400 or more; **OR**
- You had church employee income of $108.28 or more. Income from services you performed as a minister or a member of a religious order **is not** church employee income. See page SE-1.

Note: *Even if you have a loss or a small amount of income from self-employment, it may be to your benefit to file Schedule SE and use either "optional method" in Part II of Long Schedule SE. See page SE-3.*

Exception. If your only self-employment income was from earnings as a minister, member of a religious order, or Christian Science practitioner, **AND** you filed Form 4361 and received IRS approval not to be taxed on those earnings, **DO NOT** file Schedule SE. Instead, write "Exempt–Form 4361" on Form 1040, line 47.

May I Use Short Schedule SE or MUST I Use Long Schedule SE?

Did you receive wages or tips in 1993?

No

Yes

Are you a minister, member of a religious order, or Christian Science practitioner who received IRS approval **not** to be taxed on earnings from these sources, but you owe self-employment tax on other earnings? — Yes →

Was the total of your wages and tips subject to social security or railroad retirement tax **plus** your net earnings from self-employment more than $57,600? — Yes →

No

No

Are you using one of the optional methods to figure your net earnings (see page SE-3)? — Yes →

Was the total of your wages and tips subject to Medicare tax **plus** your net earnings from self-employment more than $135,000? — Yes →

No

No

Did you receive church employee income reported on Form W-2 of $108.28 or more? — Yes → No ←

Did you receive tips subject to social security or Medicare tax that you **did not** report to your employer? — Yes →

No

YOU MAY USE SHORT SCHEDULE SE BELOW

YOU MUST USE LONG SCHEDULE SE ON THE BACK

Section A—Short Schedule SE. Caution: *Read above to see if you can use Short Schedule SE.*

1	Net farm profit or (loss) from Schedule F, line 36, and farm partnerships, Schedule K-1 (Form 1065), line 15a	**1**
2	Net profit or (loss) from Schedule C, line 31; Schedule C-EZ, line 3; and Schedule K-1 (Form 1065), line 15a (other than farming). Ministers and members of religious orders see page SE-1 for amounts to report on this line. See page SE-2 for other income to report	**2**
3	Combine lines 1 and 2	**3**
4	**Net earnings from self-employment.** Multiply line 3 by 92.35% (.9235). If less than $400, **do not** file this schedule; you do not owe self-employment tax . . . . ►	**4**
5	**Self-employment tax.** If the amount on line 4 is: ● $57,600 or less, multiply line 4 by 15.3% (.153) and enter the result. ● More than $57,600 but less than $135,000, multiply the amount in excess of $57,600 by 2.9% (.029). Then, add $8,812.80 to the result and enter the total. ● $135,000 or more, enter $11,057.40. Also enter on **Form 1040, line 47. (Important:** You are allowed a deduction for **one-half** of this amount. Multiply line 5 by 50% (.5) and enter the result on **Form 1040, line 25.)**	**5**

For Paperwork Reduction Act Notice, see Form 1040 Instructions.   Cat. No. 11358Z   **Schedule SE (Form 1040) 1993**

Figure 5. Page 1 of Schedule SE, showing the short schedule used by most editorial freelancers.

Commercial Rent Tax (NYC CR-A), which is a 6 percent tax on a base rent of $21,000 or more paid on rented premises used for business purposes.

Most freelancers do not owe significant amounts on these taxes, but it is important to file the forms even if nothing is owed. Several years ago, New York City officials combed tax records for eligible taxpayers who had not filed the Commercial Rent Tax form. As a result, many freelancers received notices of several thousands of dollars owed in penalties and interest. It is therefore easier to file the form even though nothing is owed than to not file it and risk paying a fine.

On the Unincorporated Business Tax, the current rule is that if your unincorporated business income does not exceed $11,000 (after deductions), you owe no tax and you file form NYC 202 EZ. But read the directions or check with a professional tax adviser, because once you factor in all the exemptions, you won't have to pay tax if your income (after deductions) is less than $25,000. If, however, your unincorporated business income is greater than that, then you must pay the tax, using form NYC 202. Therefore, so that you can take the maximum deduction for which you qualify, it is important that you keep accurate records of all your business expenses.

The nonfiling and late-filing penalties of this form are the same and are figured on the amount of time that has elapsed between the date you should have filed and the date of your assessment. Check the directions booklet or with the New York City Department of Finance (718-935-6000) for current rates. I am told, however, that the usual penalty for nonfiling is $250, so even if you owe no tax, you should file the form.

A glimmer of hope for relief from filing these forms was offered in the report titled *Holding Our Competitive Edge: Book & Magazine Publishing in New York City,* which was released in June 1994 by Ruth W. Messinger (Manhattan Borough President), Adam Friedman (Director of Economic Development), and Judy Goldberg (then Economic Development Associate). This report suggests that the filing requirement be changed so that those who are not liable for the tax need not file the forms. It should be noted that many individuals, including some accountants, have been lobbying for this change for at least twenty years. Even though the suggestion has not been acted upon as of this writing, it is encouraging that someone high in city government has taken notice of the need.

Freelancers who live in New York City and take the home office deduction on Schedule C (see above) or rent outside office space must file Form NYC CR-A, Commercial Rent Tax. The period for this tax is from June 1 to May 31, so it is not filed in April with your other taxes. The current rule is that if the amount of your base rent subject to tax is less than $21,000 ($0 to $20,999.99), you owe nothing. You need to use the form to determine this base rent figure, but in all probability you won't owe any tax. However, if you are exempt from the tax because your base rent is less than $21,000, *and you fail to file an annual return,* a penalty of $200 will be imposed. If you should become liable for this penalty, check with your tax advisor, since there may be a way to avoid paying it.

Booklets

To help you understand and fill out the federal schedules and forms discussed in the previous section, the IRS has prepared a series of tax booklets. They are free and can be ordered by calling 1-800-829-3676 or by picking them up at an IRS office. Those booklets that would probably be most helpful to editorial freelancers who do their own taxes are listed below:

1. IRS Publication 17 (*Your Federal Income Tax*). This booklet contains a line-by-line explanation of Form 1040.
2. IRS Publication 334 (*Tax Guide for Small Businesses*). This one will help you with Schedule C.
3. IRS Publication 587 (*Business Use of the Home*). Includes information on the rules for deducting the cost of a computer.
4. IRS Publication 910 (*Guide to Free Tax Services*): Besides these services, this booklet contains a list of publications available from the IRS.

While these and other booklets will answer many of your questions, there is a Catch-22. Even though they are written and published by the IRS, if you make a mistake on your forms that is caused by an error in one or more of the booklets, the mistake is still your responsibility, and you may be held liable for interest and penalties, if any. Because they're useful, however, it's a good idea to get them anyway.

RETIREMENT PLANS

Even though retirement plans are an added expense, it is a good idea to make the sacrifice. Many freelancers do not establish such plans because they don't plan to retire. Even so, you may reach age 60 or 70 and decide that you don't want to work quite as much as you have in the past. Any monies accumulated in a retirement fund will then be a welcome supplement to your other, reduced income. Or it may happen that for some reason you're forced to retire. In such an event, you will be glad to have the retirement account funds available.

Since I am not an expert on retirement accounts, in this section I will simply mention some of the options available to independent contractors.

IRA (individual retirement account). This is one of the better known and more popular retirement plans. You can contribute up to $2000 a year as an individual; if you're a couple and both of you are working, you can each have an IRA and each contribute up to $2000 a year; if you're a couple and only one of you is working, you can contribute up to $2250 a year. Your annual contributions and interest are not taxable. IRA funds are usually invested in bank CDs, mutual funds, or money market funds. According to IRS rules, if you withdraw funds before age 59½, you may be liable for a 10 percent penalty and must pay tax on the amount withdrawn; otherwise, you can start making withdrawals after age 59½, at which time you pay tax on the amount withdrawn each year. You must begin withdrawing the money at age 70½, however, if you haven't already done so. Check with your bank for further details before signing up—this goes for any of the alternatives listed below.

SEP (single-employee pension plan or simplified employee pension plan). This plan is probably best suited for editorial freelancers since it is the only one that lists sole proprietors among the categories of businesses for which it was designed. In a SEP you can contribute up to 15 percent of earned income (i.e., your gross *professional* or self-employment income) up to a maximum contribution of $30,000 per year. The money is invested the same ways as it would be for an IRA. Any money withdrawn before age 59½ may be subject to a 10 percent penalty. Funds withdrawn after age 59½ are taxable, and you must start making withdrawals by age 70½. With the SEP you are required by the IRS to file disclosure forms each year, but this is no more difficult than filing for an IRA and can be easily handled either by you or by your tax preparer.

Keogh (pronounced key-oh). There are two types of Keogh plans, the profit sharing Keogh and the money purchase Keogh. In the profit sharing Keogh you can change the amount of the contribution from year to year—you can even skip a year. The maximum contribution is either 15 percent of your earned (i.e., gross self-employment) income or $30,000, whichever is smaller. For example, if you grossed $45,000 in professional fees one year, you could contribute up to 15 percent of it, or $6750, which is smaller than $30,000. In the money purchase Keogh you can contribute up to 25 percent of earned income or $30,000, whichever is smaller. Also, in this plan you must make a contribution every year, and this contribution must be at the percentage you first established. Keogh funds are invested pretty much the same way they are in SEPs and IRAs. If you have a profit sharing plan, hardship withdrawals are permitted.

In both types of plans, any money withdrawn before age 59½ may incur a 10 percent penalty, plus an extra 20 percent will be withheld to pay taxes. All money withdrawn from age 59½ on will be subject to income tax. If you haven't started withdrawing funds by age 70½, minimum distributions, figured according to a preset formula, will be made. The forms required by the IRS to meet the annual disclosure requirement are more complicated than those for a SEP. Thus, there is usually an administrative fee of some kind.

For more information about these and other retirement plans, talk to your financial adviser or the investment consultant at your bank or, if possible, get a copy of the following booklet, which was produced for Citibank by the Strategic Programs Group of BusinessWeek: *Citibank Retirement Guide for Small Businesses*, McGraw-Hill, New York, 1992. Or see if your bank has something comparable.

INSURANCE

Life Insurance

Although buying insurance can be likened to having a suit made by a tailor—insurance needs are no more universal than people's measurments—some advice is good for everyone. For example, most financial advisors will tell you that everyone should have life insurance plus an annuity. This is because it's better to have your retirement income in several pots rather than in only one. Also, life insurance policies, which are self-completing (i.e., come due when the policyholder dies), can be made to complement annuities, which come due when the owner reaches a particular age. For example, suppose an annuity holder also has a life insurance policy for the same amount as the annuity, say $200,000. If the holder dies at an earlier age than that specified in the annuity, the life insurance pays the beneficiary $200,000, while the $200,000 annuity remains in force until its stated expiration date.

When buying life insurance, whether it's term (expires when the holder reaches a specified age), whole (lasts the lifetime of the insured; premiums are fixed), or universal (lasts for the insured's lifetime; premiums can be variable), the buyer should opt for an amount that is ten times the primary breadwinner's salary. Then, if something should happen to the policyholder, the beneficiary has the option of converting the policy to an annuity that will generate a fixed annual income for the survivors. One thing a widow or widower will never complain about is the amount of the premiums paid for the insurance: they'll only say, "I wish we'd bought more."

After deciding on a life insurance policy, you might also consider a flexible premium retirement annuity. This is a nonqualified plan—that is, the payments are *not* tax-deductible. Since this is in the nature of an investment, there is no fixed amount that needs to be contributed each year, but each insurance company does require a minimum monthly contribution, which can be as little as $25. Ask an agent for details.

Some insurance agents might try to interest you in whole or universal variable life (VAL) insurance as a form of retirement investment. Be very careful of this one. Although these plans offer a death benefit, allow withdrawal of the cash value at any time, and permit a choice of investments within the policy, your money is invested in stocks. Therefore you can lose if stock prices decline. Also, the differential of gross profit made is taxable, but the life insurance probably won't be—it depends on the size of the person's estate. Again, ask an agent for details.

Health Insurance

Health insurance can be a problem for editorial freelancers. As independent contractors they do not qualify for group insurance rates, and it is very difficult for them to get certain types of insurance, such as disability and dental. Adding to this difficulty is the fact that major medical insurance premiums are so high that freelancers often have to opt for large deductibles, with the result that the insurance can be used only in the case of a long hospital stay or a protracted illness that may require out-patient and/or home nursing care.

Freelancers can overcome these difficulties by joining a group-rate insurance plan through a professional association. Many such associations offer medical, accident, dental, and/or disability insurance. In this instance, however, you might want to think beyond such obvious choices as editorial and publishing organizations; for example, if you're age fifty or over, there is the American Association of Retired Persons. Other large groups worth considering include, but are not limited to, the Modern Language Association and the American Association of University Women.

Before joining a professional association for its health plan, you should check to see (1) what types of insurance are available to members; (2) whether these plans are more viable and affordable than similar insurances in the public sector; and (3) what kind of care is offered. Because of their status, freelance editorial workers (but not writers) qualify for somewhat lower rates on certain types of policies, such as accident or disability. Also, if the annual premium is too large to handle at one time, most insurance companies will allow you to pay in quarterly or even monthly installments.

Most often, however, the medical and dental insurance plans offered by professional associations are health maintenance or HMO-type plans. HMOs and similar plans are becoming the norm rather than the exception in the health care field. One reason for this is that, having been alarmed by the federal government's recent attempt at passing universal health insurance legislation, insurance companies have become heavily involved in the burgeoning HMO business. Their level of involvment varies, however: in some instances they own the HMO; in other cases they sign contracts with preferred-provider organizations (PPOs). PPOs are comprehensive plans, usually offered to employees of corporations, in which insurees can (within certain limits) choose their own physicians and hospitals.

In some HMOs members must use the HMO's employed physicians; in others, members have the option of seeing private doctors or doctors licensed by the HMO. Freelancers therefore need to look at the various available HMOs to determine differences in cost and degree of freedom in choosing a physician. They should also find out whether there is a mechanism for going outside the HMO for care while still being covered by it, and whether there is a copayment or small deductible when the freelancer does opt to go outside the plan.

Most freelancers who have Blue Cross/Blue Shield have kept it after leaving a full-time in-house job. Since Blue Cross hasn't made group rates available to many types of associations, it may be difficult for you to get this form of insurance on your own. In New York State, Blue Cross also tends to have a high premium and to be granted frequent premium increases. Since each state has its own Blue Cross organization, however, this may not be true in your area. In some locations Blue Cross has open enrollment periods during which individuals can join, but before you sign up, check their financial status (some Blue Cross companies are at financial risk) and what is offered.

Finally, the bad news is that since insurance companies are such a powerful lobbying force, there probably will be little relief from high premiums and premium increases for the foreseeable future, especially since the federal government seems disinclined to legislate a universally affordable health care plan.

The discussions in the previous three chapters on the major financial realities of a freelancer's life bring to a close our investigation of the business of editorial freelancing. There are, however, a few other topics that will be of interest to editorial freelancers—after dinner mints, as it were. These are discussed in the next and final chapter.

LAST THOUGHTS 10

Because the preceding chapters could not comfortably consider everything of interest to editorial freelancers, I have gathered together a few additional topics in this chapter. These are discussed briefly in the following sections.

RUMINATIONS ON WHY EDITORS EDIT

So why do editors do what they do? Basically, it's because they are people who love and care passionately about language. It is editors who are on the front lines in the struggle to preserve the niceties and subtle distinctions expressed by the words we use: *comprise* vs. *compose; currently* vs. *presently; which* vs. *that; classic* vs. *classical*, to name a few. English is an incredibly rich and vibrant language comprising words with roots in many other languages, including French, Spanish, German, Italian, and Latin. It is this richness and diversity that editors seek to preserve.

If it's for the love of language that editors go into their chosen profession, what keeps them in it is their ability to use this love and understanding to help authors express themselves in the clearest possible terms so the reader can better understand what's being said. In other words, editors serve the author and the reader by acting as a bridge between them.

Elizabeth Whalen, a technical writer/editor, has reduced this process to what she calls "the editing equation" so noneditorial people can better understand what it is that editors do: $x + y + z =$ editing, where x is "concern for the reader," y is "support for authors," and z is "value for the company or client."[1] "Value for the company or client"—now there's a concept we don't hear or think about very often, we're so busy worring about the other two. But what does it mean? Whalen answers this question in the following terms: making the documents produced by the company as clear, accurate, and easy to read as possible. Documents that do not comprise all three of these criteria may call the accuracy of the document and the company's integrity into question in the reader's mind. Thus, a client may be lost.

It is therefore the business of every editorial freelancer to be the best he or she can be. Since freelancers get so little positive feedback from authors and clients, holding high standards can be frustrating. As can the shortcuts forced by tight schedules and such statements as, "No. Leave it. No one but us is going to notice anyway." But frustration, or the fatigue it causes, is no reason to let standards slip.

Besides discussing the business of editorial freelancing, this book has also touched on the "freelance personality." Although freelancers at times have been characterized as having a "victim psychology" and the "editorial personality" as sometimes being alienating, I have found the majority of editorial freelancers to be highly intelligent, articulate, and dedicated individuals. Which is another reason why it's so stimulating and satisfying to work in this field—the people you come in contact with.

CROSSING OVER

Many theatrical performers suffer from type-casting and so, in a sense, do editorial freelancers. For the latter, the stereotype may be as difficult to break out of as it is for an actor who always plays the heavy to land a role as the romantic lead. This is because staff editors are reluctant to give a work of fiction to a freelancer whose specialty is math and computers or an el-hi textbook to one who has been editing college textbooks. Nor is a book editor likely to get an assignment from a magazine. This reluctance is due, of course, to the differences between the editorial requirements of each of the categories. The one time I copyedited an el-hi textbook, the result was less than satisfactory from the client's point of view. Their major complaint: "You didn't ask enough questions." (A college textbook editor starts from the premise that the author knows the field, and therefore doesn't question much of the content. In contrast, an el-hi editor is supposed to query every fact and detail.)

The difficulties in going from proofreading to copyediting, from copyediting to line editing, or from editing to writing are not as great, because each of these specialties includes elements of one or more of the others. That is, a proofreader must have much of the knowledge and many of the skills required of a copyeditor; a copyeditor must develop the skills necessary to do line editing; an editor often has to write or rewrite portions of a manuscript as well as have knowledge of how a book is organized and constructed. But a person who specializes in editing college textbooks won't have developed all the skills necessary for editing a novel or a magazine article. Therefore it can be difficult to find a client who will take a chance and assign a freelancer a project outside of his or her specialty area.

The easiest and most obvious way of effecting such a change would be to take a course. Say you're a textbook editor and you want to expand into working for magazines. If you take a course in magazine writing or editing, chances are you'll not only gain the necessary knowledge to cross over, but you'll probably meet some people who can help you make the change.

Another alternative would be to seek work on a professional journal, or, if one of your specialties is computers, on a computer magazine. Thus when you approach the popular magazine you are aiming at, you will be able to show some experience in a "related" area.

Since an experienced copyeditor who specializes in math and physics is often able to successfully copyedit books on subjects as diverse as business management and cookie/cracker manufacturing, some clients will offer a favorite freelancer projects outside that person's area of expertise. Although my first book for Scribner was on quarks (particle physics is one of my specialty areas), succeeding jobs included such nonspecialty-related subjects as Hollywood costume designers, wooden boat design, the male reproductive system, retirement planning, and the prevention of miscarriage. In other words, once a client likes your work, some of the subject restrictions may no longer be strictly applied.

All I'm suggesting is that, although you will hear that it's very difficult for a technical editor to find nontechnical work, or for someone who does magazine editing to get work editing a textbook, or to move from adult to juvenile (or vice versa), it is not impossible—and often involves less effort than you'd think. And now that I've illustrated a couple of ways in which you can move from one area of editorial work to another, you can probably find others.

FREELANCE RITUALS

It could be successfully argued that freelance rituals have only a peripheral bearing on the business of editorial freelancing. I decided to include some of them here, however, because the results of a recent survey of editorial freelancers suggest that rituals are an important aspect of many freelancers' lives. Since I tend to keep mine secret for fear of ridicule, I thought it might make us all feel easier to know that we're not alone in this indulgence. In fact, whatever rationale you attach to your rituals—"It's a reward for working late at night"; "I can't work effectively unless I ———" —they can be viewed as just another tool we use to help us get the job done, and so we shouldn't feel guilty or strange about them. I have therefore compiled a list of fourteen such rituals (some might say eccentricities).

1. A frequent freelance ritual is that of wearing the same garments (though not always the same undergarments) for a week at a time or for the duration of a project. I must confess to being a practitioner of this one, occasionally carrying it over into my everyday attire in that I always wear one of two or three neckties because I consider them lucky.
2. Another attire-related ritual is wearing a certain article of clothing, such as a beret, or a certain color, such as purple, during working hours. For many freelancers, the colors they wear or are surrounded by while working are important to their sense of well-being. Comfort also plays a part in the clothing rituals, many freelancers preferring workout suits or other forms of casual, loose-fitting clothing.
3. Some freelancers exercise before, during, and/or after work. This might include running, swimming, yoga, exercise machines, or weight lifting. Besides its ritualistic aspects, working out on a regular basis is not a bad idea for freelancers, who lead an essentially sedentary lifestyle. For example, I find the stretching exercises of yoga especially effective for keeping my body limber and preventing back problems.

4. Many dog-owning freelancers start the day by taking the dog for a long walk. Others take regular breaks throughout the day to play with a puppy or a cat.

5. Some freelancers start their workday by cleaning off their desks; others end theirs by setting up their work for the next morning's labor.

6. Another favorite ritual is snacking—in fact, one freelancer said that when he began freelancing he might as well have moved his typewriter into the refrigerator! Many freelancers feel as if their jaw muscles are wired into the process of writing, editing, or proofreading, and that they work better while they're munching. The type of snack consumed is also important. I knew one freelancer who favored a mixture of peanuts and raisins. (I once tried using this addictive concoction, but stopped when I began gaining weight.) For others, the preferred snack is cinnamon graham crackers, Granola bars, or cinnamon buns. Sometimes the brand of the snack is crucial: Nabisco works, Keebler doesn't, or vice versa.

7. Almost all freelancers need to be drinking some type of beverage while they work—for me it's herb teas, and always in a specific order. Other freelancers can't work without coffee, water, or some kind of soft drink.

8. Quite a few freelancers, myself included, listen to music while they work. For example, like many other freelancers, I prefer classical or operatic music because I can't concentrate when I can understand what's being sung, as in pop music or show tunes.

9. Some freelancers habitually start their days by reading a newspaper. A few even go so far as to cut out the sensational or humorous headlines and pin them up by their desks.

10. Many freelancers shut off the phone around noon in order to relax undisturbed while eating lunch and watching a favorite soap opera or series rerun on TV. On a recent episode of TV's prime time show *Homicide: Life on the Street,* one of the characters said, "I wish they'd bring back *Hawaii Five-O*." I second the motion: "Book 'im, Danno! Murder one."

11. Sharpening pencils is another common freelance ritual. Some sharpen several before they start work; others

sharpen only one so they'll be forced to periodically visit the sharpener throughout the day; and a few (like myself) postpone sharpening until finishing a section or a chapter. I also often try to make a stub last until I complete a certain portion. Whatever the case, sharp pencils are a necessity for editing and proofreading—I've sometimes likened them in my mind to scalpels because both editors and surgeons perform exacting procedures of incision, substitution, and removal.

12. Many freelancers start or finish the day with a shower, perhaps in recognition of the number of days they've been wearing the same clothes. In the morning, a shower is a good place to ruminate or plan the day's activities; afternoon showers are relaxing. In either case, the shower serves as a kind of air lock, aiding in the transition from relaxation mode to work mode, or vice versa.

13. Another related ritual is meditation before work. It's a great way to clear the mind, relax the body, and prepare for the day.

14. The final ritual is tied to modern technology—to wit, reading and answering E-mail. This can be very seductive, very relaxing, and you feel as though you're clearing a thicket before settling into the day's routine.

CURRENT TRENDS

Finally, a few words on current trends in the publishing industry and how they affect editorial freelancing.

The first trend, which continues from the 1970s, is that of consolidation, a process whereby the large companies get larger by assimilating smaller companies. This trend has slowed considerably, however, due to the dearth of companies left to acquire. Still, since some large corporations, such as Raytheon, may eventually decide their publishing holdings don't fit their overall corporate structure and put them on the market, and since large conglomerates still acquire the occasional successful small press, we can't say that this trend has now ended.

Paralleling consolidations is the continual establishment of small presses to fill various subject niches. These niches occur because publishers that have been acquired by larger corporations, and are therefore influenced by the bottom line, no longer find these areas profitable. One of these newly available areas, oddly enough, is new fiction. That is, beginning writers are finding it easier to sell their work to small presses, which are in turn interested in developing new talent, than to the more established houses. These new companies are often badly in need of editorial freelancers, particularly those who specialize in a press's subject area. While most of these presses are listed in LMP, the Small Press Center in New York also publishes a directory (see Appendix C3).

At the same time that consolidation is occurring, so is downsizing, caused by publishers' desire to reduce production costs. Downsizing generally happens in one of two ways. First, when one publishing company is acquired by another, or when a corporation that already owns one publishing company acquires another, the staffs are eventually merged, which means that redundant positions—eight rather than four project editors, for example—are eliminated. In this case, three or four of the eight will be let go. But the company may later decide to reduce staff further, which is when the second wave of downsizing occurs. The company may have decided to do less of the production work in-house, relying more on total-concept houses and freelancers. Thus more jobs can be eliminated, forcing more people to enter the freelance market, either temporarily or permanently. One consequence of this is more freelancers competing for the same jobs. Another is that as companies continue to downsize, the work available to freelancers will be at increasingly higher levels. In other words, where copyediting and proofreading now make up the majority of the jobs, the number of freelance developmental and project editing assignments will increase. In any case, downsizing creates more freelance opportunities, since someone also needs to do the various tasks that were formerly handled by in-house staff members.

Another trend is toward more electronic editing. While much editing is still done on hard copy, and many of the traditional production practices continue to be followed, there is a growing demand for freelancers who are computer literate and have computer capabilities in a wide variety of areas. This is because an increasing amount of work is being done on-line, or through the Internet. These trends are abetted by computers, fax machines, and modems, all of which make it easy for publishers to communicate and exchange documents with freelancers, and vice versa. At the present time, however, all is not as simple in telecommunications as some of the advertising would have us believe. Among other difficulties, the failure of in-house people to inform the at-home worker of such vital information as sudden schedule changes—information that used to be imparted when two people happened to pass in the hall or had cubicles close enough so that visiting was easy. Still, some companies, such as AT&T, are insisting that their staff members work at least one day out of five at home. In any event, areas of electronic editorial work will continue to expand as new technologies become available.

Publishing companies and especially magazines are locating or relocating outside of traditional publishing centers like New York, Boston, and San Francisco, a trend that is being facilitated by the new technologies. These same technologies make it possible for freelancers to have an international as well as intranational clientele. But this also means that some of these companies are moving closer to freelancers who live in areas far removed from traditional publishing centers, giving them easier access to both current and potential clients. Unless some changes are made, the increasing cost of operating in large metropolitan areas will continue to force publishers to move out of these publishing centers, further diminishing the quality of life in some of our larger cities. Already, the school divisions of most major publishers are now located in the suburbs—for example, in Boston the only one left in the city proper is Houghton Mifflin. One effect of this continuing exodus will be a reduced number of publishers drawing on the same large pool of local freelancers. This will mean that freelancers will have to look outside their immediate locations for clients, as well as forcing them to become, however reluctantly, technologically proficient.

Although this cannot be classified as a trend, I think it's worth mentioning that I've been hearing an increasing number of freelancers commenting that there seem to be fewer freelance jobs available, especially in medical writing and copyediting. While this can perhaps be traced to the recent closing of several medical magazines, what these freelancers may also be experiencing is the first pinch of the increased competition referred to earlier in this section. More freelancers competing for the same jobs. Still, it might not be too much of a reach to say that on the whole these trends suggest a bullish future for editorial freelancers and freelance work.

NOTES

1. Elizabeth Whalen, "The Editing Equation: A Reply to Authors Who Ask, `How Come You Changed My Stuff?'," *Technical Communications*, vol. 39, no. 3, Third Quarter, August 1992, p. 329.

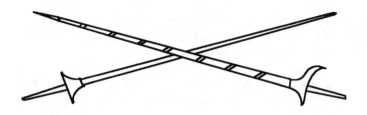

APPENDIX A
Sample Copyediting Test

The following pages* represent a copyediting test that might be presented to a freelancer applying for a job copyediting scientific subjects.

IMPAIRED TEMPORAL RESOLUTION IN DEVELOPMENTAL DYSLEXIA

Peter H. Wolff

The outcome variables for the first set of studies were (a) variability or inter-response intervals (IRI) reported as standard deviations for each finger (in msec); (2) mean tapping frequency over a trial relative to metronome rate, as a general measure of the subject's ability to maintain the prescribed response frequency; and (3) the ratio of response by the left and right fingers over a trial, as a global measure of the subject's ability to preserve the prescribed bimanual pattern throughout a trial. In most of the studies

*These pages are reproduced here with the kind permission of The New York Academy of Sciences.

conventional analyses of variance on grouped data were used to test for group differences. Subsequently, more refined qualitative analyses were introduced to examine <u>how</u>, as well as <u>how well</u>, individual aubjects performed the bimanual tasks.

To locate the specific findings in a larger context, I begin with a summary of the results:

1. Dyslexic individuals performed the bimanual tasks with significantly greater variability of IRI than age matched controls in each of the age groups tested, (p< .01; .001) ; they also deviated more from the prescribed response frequency.

2. Pathological controls did not differ from controls, but like normal controls they differed significantly from dyslexic subjects.

3. The various tasks were not equall discriminating at each age: a) None of the dyslexic students differed from controls on analogous <u>unimanual</u> tapping tasks, ; b) nine-ten year old dyslexic students differed from controls on bimanual <u>synchronous</u> tapping tasks that were no longer discriminating at 11-13 years (see figure 1).

REFERENCE

1. Coltheart, M., J. Masterson, et al. 1983 Surface dyslexia. <u>Quart. J. Exp. Psychol.</u>, <u>35A</u>: 469-495.
2. Tallal, P., R. Stark & D. Mellits. 1985. The relationship between auditory temporal analysis and receptive language development. <u>Neuropsychol.</u>, <u>23</u>: 527-534.
3. Livingston, M. S., G. D. Rosen, F. W. Drislane & A. M. Galaburda. 1991. Physiological and anatomical evidence for a magnocellular defect in developmental dyslexia. <u>Proc. Natl.Acad. Sci.</u>, <u>88</u>: 7943-7947.
4. Lovegrove, W. J., R. P. Garzia & S. B. Nicholson. 1990. Experimental evidence for a transient system deficit in specific reading disability. <u>J. Amer. Opotmet. Assoc.</u>, <u>61</u>: 137-146.
5. Hanes, M. L. 1986. Rhythm as a factor of mediated and nonmediated processing reading. In J.R. Evans & M. Clynes (Eds.) , <u>Rhythm in Psychological, Linguistic and Musical Processes</u>. C.C. Thomas. Springfield, IL.

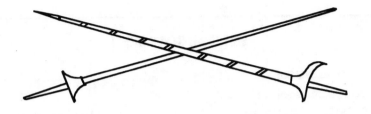

APPENDIX B
Sample Style Sheet

This sample shows how a typical style sheet might be filled in. The entries are the kinds of things that could be included in a style sheet. Not all style sheets are typed, however; freelancers often turn in the same style sheet that they compiled during the editing process. Usually in a recopied or typed style sheet the words and phrases on pages 2 and 3 would be organized alphabetically within each letter.

EDITORIAL STYLE SHEET

AUTHOR <u>Smith & Williams</u>   ____ DATE STARTED

TITLE <u>Universal Universalities</u>   ____ DATE COMPLETED

PRODUCTION EDITOR <u>Edith Editor</u>   <u>Frieda Freelancer</u> COPY EDITOR

Instructions to Copy Editor:

Please be sure you are familiar with the use of this form before starting your copy editing assignment. Enter on the style sheet all items that may require verification during subsequent stages of production. If you need more space for a given category, use adjacent unneeded space, but change headings so that they will be applicable. Use extra sheets or pages if necessary.

The style sheet will ordinarily be a rough worksheet; unless it is unusually neat and readable so that it can easily be used by others, the information it contains should be transferred to a clean form before the manuscript is turned in.

NUMBERS AND DATES

Spell out one through nine, except per
  Chicago: three weeks, but 10-week period

5 percent; 5% in tables and math

1200; 12,000

1970s

nineteenth century

30°C (no space); 273 K (degrees kelvin)

ABBREVIATIONS

i.e., e.g., etc. in parens; spell in text

U.S. as adjective; spell as a noun

no end periods for units of measure,
  except in.

PPI = producer price index

FCOJ = frozen concentrated orange juice

ARP = acreage reduction program

CERN = European Center for Nuclear Research

mmHg = millimeters of mercury

WIMP = weakly interacting massive particle

PUNCTUATION

serial comma

Rogers's (<u>Chicago</u> 6.24)

punctuate displayed equations

TABULAR MATTER

table footnotes take superscript italic
  lowercase letters

CAPITALIZATION HYPHENATION SPELLING ITALICS
 	
Indicate the following and other abbreviations when appropriate:
 	
(n) noun
(v) verb
(a) adj preceding noun
(pa) predicate adj
(col) collective nouns
(s) singular
(pl) plural
	A
	
	a priori
	anti-inflationary
	antipersonnel
		B
		
		black body (n & a)
		bremsstrahlung
		broad range
		best-fit (a)
		breakeven (n);
		  break-even (a)
			C
			
			cancer-risk (a)
			cathode-ray tube
			Chapter 6 in text
			  and in parens

D disc data base data are deutsche mark	**E** ensure excited-state (a) Eurodollars	**F** Figure 7.8 (Fig. 7.8 in parens) free-air (a) federal	**G** Gedankenexperiment government-owned (a)
H half-life high energy (n & a) hog slaughter (n & a)	**I-J-K** in utero inflation-adjusted (a)	**L** least-action principle	**M** multi-indicator multicollinearity model-predicted

N	O	P-Q	PERMISSIONS REQUIRED
nonnumerical nonfatal	oil-consuming (a)	pathlength power-series (a) per capita price/earnings	(Use this column to list numbers of pages containing nonoriginal matter for which permissions may be required.)

R	S	T
re-radiation round-off (a) raison d'être reexport	spin-orbit (a) supply-demand sweet-sour	two-body (a) type-II error

U-V	W	X-Y-Z
vibration-rotation variable supply (n & a) up-bow (n)	wavelength worst-case (a) whole-body (a)	X-ray (a); X ray (n) y-plane; x-y plane

BIBLIOGRAPHY STYLE

Richard P. Feynman, Robert B. Leighton,
and Matthew Sands, The Feynman Lectures
on Physics, Addison-Wesley, Reading, Mass.,
1963.

E. Foster, "Field-Level Measurements of Land
Productivity and Program Slippage."
American Journal of Agricultural Economics
75: 181–189 (1993).

FOOTNOTE STYLE

number footnotes consecutively in each
chapter

GENERAL NOTES ON TYPOGRAPHY

Mark all dashes and mark to close up when necessary

Mark paragraph indents as necessary

Mark all text boldface to avoid ambiguity

Comp will be instructed to set text italics as typed or marked

Use italics for emphasis and introduced terms

Use quotes for words as words (Chicago 6.76) and for coined words

Use boldface for all terms to be used in Glossary

MISCELLANEOUS NOTES

contractions OK

(Hint: The . . .)

check all x-refs

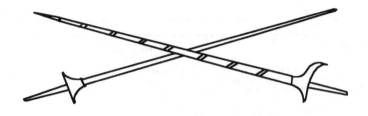

APPENDIX C
Some Resources for Freelancers*

C1: Books and Publications

Bernstein, Theodore M., *The Careful Writer, A Modern Guide to English Usage*, Atheneum, New York, 1977.

Bonura, Larry S., *The Art of Indexing*, John Wiley & Sons., New York, 1994.

Brande, Dorothea, *Becoming a Writer* (Foreword by John Gardner), J. P. Tarcher, Los Angeles, 1981.

Buchman, Dian Dincin, and Seli Groves, *The Writer's Digest Guide to Manuscript Formats*, Writer's Digest Books, Cincinnati, Ohio, 1987.

Career Directory Series, The Career Press Inc., P.O. Box 34, Hawthorne, NJ 07507.

Cook, Claire Kehrwald, *Line by Line, How to Improve Your Own Writing*, Houghton Mifflin Co., Boston, 1985.

Copy Editor, The National Newsletter for Professional Copy Editors, P.O. Box 604, Ansonia Station, New York, NY 10023-0604.

The Editorial Eye, Editorial Experts, Inc., 66 Canal Center Plaza, Suite 200, Alexandria, VA 22314-1538.

---

* Some of the citations in Appendixes C1 and C2, and the majority of the information in Appendix C3 was provided by Jan Hall, Senior Editor, Glencoe Publishing, Westerville, Ohio.

Editorial Freelancers Association Professional Practices Survey, Editorial Freelancers Association, New York, 1994.

EFA Newsletter, Editorial Freelancers Association, 71 West 23rd Street, Suite 1504, New York, NY, 10010.

Freelance Editorial Association Code of Fair Practice, Freelance Editorial Association, Cambridge, Mass., 1991.

Freelance Editorial Association News, Freelance Editorial Association, Cambridge, Mass.

Fulton, Len, Ed., *International Directory of Little Magazines and Small Presses* (29th, rev. ed.), Dustbooks, Paradise, Calif., 1992.

George, Kathi (Compiler), *69 Workshops for Copy Editors, Copy Editor, The National Newsletter for Professional Copy Editors,* New York, 1994.

Gilpatrick, Eleanor, *Grants for Nonprofit Organizations, A Guide to Funding and Grant Writing,* Praeger, Westport, Conn., 1989.

Godfrey, Patricia M., *Grammatical Gleanings, Occasional Essays on Matters Grammatical, Syntactical, Idiomatic, Semantic, and Stylistic,* Editorial Freelancers Association, New York, 1993.

Grants and Awards Available to American Writers 1994/1995 (18th ed.), PEN American Center, New York, 1994.

Gross, Gerald, Ed., *Editors on Editing, What Writers Need to Know about What Editors Do* (3rd ed.), Grove Press, New York, 1993.

Guiley, Rosemary, *Career Opportunities for Writers* (2nd ed.), Facts on File Publications, New York, 1990.

Hodges, John C., et al., *Harbrace College Handbook* (12th ed.), Harcourt Brace Jovanovich, Fort Worth, Tex., 1993.

Johnson, Curt, Ed., *Who's Who in Writers, Editors & Poets: United States & Canada 1994-1995* (5th ed.), December Press, Highland Park, Ill., 1994.

Judd, Karen, *Copyediting, A Practical Guide* (2nd ed.), Crisp Publications, Los Altos, Calif., 1991.

Kaye, Judith S., and Matthew T. Crosson, *A Guide to Small Claims Court, New York State Unified Court System* (rev. April 1993), State of New York Office of Court Administration, New York, 1993.

Kohl, Martin, *The Freelancer's Bookshelf,* Editorial Freelancers Association, New York, 1994.

Lee, Marshall, Ed., *Bookmaking, The Illustrated Guide to Design/Production/Editing* (rev. & enlarged ed.), R. R. Bowker Co., New York, 1980.

McCormack, Thomas, *The Fiction Editor, the Novel, and the Novelist,* St. Martin's Press, New York, 1994.

Martin, Douglas, *Book Design,* Van Nostrand Reinhold, New York, 1989.

Messinger, Ruth W., Adam Friedman, and Judy Goldberg, *Holding Our Competitive Edge: Book & Magazine Publishing in New York City,* Office of the Manhattan Borough President, New York, June 1994.

Mulvany, Nancy, *Indexing Books,* University of Chicago Press, Chicago, 1994.

1993/94 Directory of Publications Resources, Selected Books, Periodicals, Software, Courses, Organizations, Contests, Grammar Hotlines, and Tools, Editorial Experts, Alexandria, Va., 1993.

Occupational Hazards, Problems Frequently Encountered by Freelancers, Editorial Freelancers Association, New York, 1991.

One Book/Five Ways: The Publishing Procedures of Five University Presses, University of Chicago Press, Chicago, 1994.

O'Neill, Carol L., and Avima Ruder, *The Complete Guide to Editorial Freelancing,* Barnes & Noble Books, New York, 1979. (Out of Print)

Pocket Pal, A Graphic Arts Production Handbook (13th ed.), International Paper Co., New York, 1983.

Publishers Weekly, 249 West 17th Street, New York, NY 10011.

Rogers, Geoffrey, *Editing for Print,* Writer's Digest Books, Cincinnati, Ohio. (Out of Print)

Ross-Larson, Bruce, *Edit Yourself, A Manual for Everyone Who Works with Words,* W. W. Norton, New York, 1985.

Sabin, William A., *The Gregg Reference Manual* (7th ed.), Glencoe, Columbus, Ohio, 1992.

Scholarly Publishing, A Journal for Authors & Publishers, University of Toronto Press, 10 St. Mary St., Suite 700, Toronto, Ontario, Canada M4Y 2W8.

Sharpe, Leslie T., and Irene Gunther, *Editing Fact and Fiction, A Concise Guide to Book Editing,* Cambridge University Press, New York, 1994.

Smith, Carolyn, with Jeannine Ciliotta, *Textbook Development as an Art and a Science,* Editorial Freelancers Association, New York, 1994.

Smith, Peggy, *Mark My Words, Instruction & Practice in Proofreading* (2nd ed.), Editorial Experts, Alexandria, Va., 1993. ,

————, *Simplified Proofreading: How to Catch Errors Using Fewer Marks,* Editorial Experts, Alexandria, Va., 1991.

Stern, Adrian, Ed., *CPA's Complete Billing and Collection Handbook,* Harcourt Brace, San Diego, 1993.

Tips for Successful Freelancing, Editorial Freelancers Association, New York, 1992.

Trade Names Dictionary, Gale Research Co., 835 Penobscot Bldg., Detroit, MI 48226-4094.

Venolia, Jan, *Write Right!* (rev. ed.), Ten Speed Press, Berkeley, Calif., 1988.

Volunteer Lawyers for the Arts, *National Directory* (9th ed.), New York, 1994.

White, Virginia P., *Grants for the Arts,* Plenum Press, New York, 1980.

C2: Some Organizations of Interest to Freelancers

Following is a list of organizations that might be of interest to editorial workers in general and editors, proofreaders, and writers in particular. It is by no means a complete list; for one thing it doesn't include the many writers' groups that focus on specific areas, such as romance and travel writing. For a more complete list, see the Book Trade & Allied Associations section in *Literary Market Place* and the *1993/94 Directory of Publications Resources.*

American Book Producers Association
160 Fifth Avenue
New York, NY 10010
Tel.: 212-645-2368

American Medical Writers Association (AMWA)
9650 Rockville Pike
Bethesda, MD 20814-3998
Tel.: 301-493-0003

American Society of Indexers (ASI)
PO Box 386
Port Aransas, TX 78373
Tel.: 512-749-4052; FAX: 512-749-6334

American Society of Journalists and Authors (ASJA)
1501 Broadway
Suite 302
New York, NY 10036
Tel.: 212-997-0947; FAX: 212-768-7414

Arizona Authors' Association
3509 East Shea Boulevard
Suite 117
Phoenix, AZ 85028-3339
Tel.: 602-996-9706

Associated Business Writers of America, Inc.
1450 South Havana Street
Suite 620
Aurora, CO 80012
Tel.: 303-751-7844; FAX: 303-751-8593

Association of Desk-Top Publishers (AD-TP)
4677 30th Street
Suite 800
San Diego, CA 92116-3245
Tel.: 619-563-9714; FAX: 619-280-3778

Authors Guild
330 West 42nd Street
New York, NY 10036
Tel.: 212-563-5904

The Authors League of America, Inc.
330 West 42nd Street
New York, NY 10036
Tel.: 212-564-8350; FAX: 212-564-8363

Bay Area Editors' Forum
3145 Geary Boulevard.
Box 222
San Francisco, CA 94118

Brooklyn Writers' Network (BWN)
2509 Avenue "K"
Brooklyn, NY 11210
Tel.: 718-377-4945

Canadian Authors Association
275 Slater Street
Suite 500
Ottawa, ON K1P 5H9
Canada
Tel.: 613-238-2846; FAX: 613-235-8237

Chicago Women in Publishing
43 East Ohio
Suite 914
Chicago, IL 60611
Tel.: 312-641-6311

Copywriters Council of America (CCA) - Freelance
Linick Building 102
7 Putter Lane
Middle Island, NY 11953-0102
Tel.: 516-924-8555, ext 203; FAX: 516-924-3890

Editorial Freelancers Association, Inc. (EFA)
71 West 23rd Street
Suite 1504
New York, NY 10010
Tel.: 212-929-5400; FAX: 212-929-5439

Electronic Publishing Special Interest Group (EPSIG)
% OCLC
6565 Frantz Road
Dublin, OH 43017-3395
Tel.: 614-764-6195; 800-848-5878, ext 6195
FAX: 614-764-6096

Florida Freelance Writers Association
Affiliate of Cassell Network of Writers
Box 9844
Fort Lauderdale, FL 33310
Tel.: 305-485-0795; 800-351-9278
FAX: 305-485-0806

Freelance Editorial Association (FEA)
Box 835
Cambridge, MA 02238
Tel.: 617-729-8164

Freelance Editors' Association of Canada (FEAC)
35 Spadina Road
Toronto, ON M5R 2S9
Canada
Tel.: 416-975-1379; FAX: 416-975-1839

Illinois Writers, Inc.
Illinois State University
English Department % Jim Elledge
Normal, IL 61761-6901
Tel.: 309-438-7705

Independent Writers of Chicago
7855 Gross Point Road
Suite M
Skokie, IL 60077
Tel.: 708-676-784

Independent Writers of Southern California
3625 South Glendon Avenue
Suite 107
Los Angeles, CA 90034
Tel.: 310-470-9654; FAX: 714-675-0609
(Mailing Address: Box 34518, Los Angeles, CA 90034)

International Black Writers (IBW)
Box 1030
Chicago, IL 60690
Tel.: 312-924-3818

League of Vermont Writers
Box 1058
Waitsfield, VT 05673
Tel.: 802-496-3271

Maine Writers and Publishers Alliance
12 Pleasant Street
Brunswick, ME 04011
Tel.: 207-729-6333

Media Alliance
Fort Mason Center
Building D
San Francisco, CA 94123
Tel.: 415-441-2557

National Association for Young Writers
215 Valle del Sol Drive
Santa Fe, NM 87501
Tel.: 505-982-8596

National Association of Desktop Publishers (NADTP)
462 Old Boston Street
Topsfield, MA 01983
Tel.: 800-874-4113; FAX: 508-887-6117

National Federation of Abstracting & Information Services
(NFAIS)
1429 Walnut Street
Philadelphia, PA 19102
Tel.: 215-563-2406; FAX: 215-563-2848

National Writers Union
873 Broadway
Suite 203
New York, NY 10003
Tel.: 212-254-0279; FAX: 212-254-0673

Nebraska Writers Guild, Inc.
Box 30341
Lincoln, NE 68503-0341
Tel.: 402-477-3804

The Newsletter Association
1401 Wilson Boulevard
Suite 207
Arlington, VA 22209
Tel.: 703-527-2333; 800-356-9302
FAX: 703-841-0629

PEN American Center
Division of International PEN
568 Broadway
New York, NY 10012
Tel.: 212-334-1660; FAX: 212-334-2181

PEN Center USA West
672 South Lafayette Park Place
Suite 41
Los Angeles, CA 90057
Tel.: 213-365-8500; FAX: 213-365-9616

Professional Editors Network (PEN)
Box 19265
Minneapolis, MN 55419-0265
Tel.: 612-647-1210

Proofreaders Club of New York
38-15 149 Street
Flushing, NY 11354

Publication Services Guild (PSG)
PO Box 19663
Atlanta, GA 30325
Tel.: 404-525-0985

San Diego Professional Editors' Network (SD/PEN)
4657 Cajon Way
San Diego, CA 92115
Tel.: 619-286-1591

Society for Scholarly Publishing
10200 West 44th Avenue
Suite 304
Wheat Ridge, CO 80033
Tel.: 303-422-3914; FAX: 303-422-8894

Society of American Business Editors & Writers (SABEW)
℅ Janine Latus-Musick
University of Missouri
PO Box 838
Columbia, MO 65205
Tel.: 314-882-7862

The Society of Editors
PO Box 176
Carlton South
Victoria 3050, Australia

Society of Freelance Editors and Proofreaders
℅ Kathleen Lyle
43 Brighton Terrace Road
Sheffield S10 1NT
United Kingdom

The Society of Midland Authors
152 North Scoville,
Oak Park, IL 60302
Tel.: 708-383-7568; FAX: 708-524-9233

The Society of Southwestern Authors (SSA)
Box 30355
Tucson, AZ 85751-0355
Tel.: 602-299-3523

Space Coast Writers Guild
Box 804
Melbourne, FL 32902
Tel.: 305-727-0051

Texas Writers Association
219 Preston Royal Shopping Center No. 3
Dallas, TX 75230
Tel.: 214-363-9979

Washington Independent Writers (WIW)
220 Woodward Building
733 15th Street NW
Washington, DC 20005
Tel.: 202-347-4973; FAX: 202-628-0298

Women in Scholarly Publishing (WISP)
Indiana University Press
601 North Morton Street
Bloomington, IN 47404-3797
Tel.: 812-855-2752; FAX: 812-855-7931

Writers Alliance
Box 2014
Setauket, NY 11733
Tel.: 516-751-7080

C3: Other Services of Interest to Freelancers

Courses and Workshops

Following is a list of some of the many organizations and institutions that sponsor courses and workshops of interest to editorial workers. Note, however, that since this list does not cite specific courses, you should consult one of the following sources for further information: *69 Workshops for Copy Editors,* compiled by Kathi George and published by *Copy Editor, The National Newsletter for Professional Copy Editors,* P.O. Box 604, Ansonia Station, New York, NY 10023-0604; the *1993/94 Directory of Publications Resources;* or the institution itself.

American University
Professional Development Workshops in Writing and Editing
Washington, DC 20016

Association of Graphic Arts
The Evening School
5 Penn Plaza
New York, NY 10001
(212) 279-2100

City University of New York (CUNY)
Graduate Center
Education and Publishing Program
Office of Special Programs
33 West 42nd Street
New York, NY 10036
(212) 575-1493

Council for Advancement and Support of Education (CASE)
11 Dupont Circle
Suite 400
Washington, DC 20036
(202) 328-5900

editcetera
1845-A Berkeley Way
Berkeley, CA 94703
(510) 849-1110

Editorial Experts Training Service
66 Canal Center Plaza
Suite 200
Alexandria, VA 22314
(703) 683-7453

Editorial Freelancers Association
71 West 23rd Street
Suite 1504
New York, NY 10010
(212) 929-5400

Georgetown University
Professional Development Program in Editing and Publications
Washington, DC 20057
(202) 687-6153

Graphic Arts Education Center
Graphic Arts Association
Local Chapter of Printing Industries of America
1900 Cherry Street
Philadelphia, PA 19103
(215) 299-3300

Howard University Press
Book Publishing Institute
2900 Van Ness Street NW
Washington, DC 20008
(202) 686-6498

Massachusetts Institute of Technology
Summer Session Office
Building E19, Room 356
Cambridge, MA 02139
(617) 253-2101

New York University
School of Continuing Education
Management Institute
48 Cooper Square
Room 108
New York, NY 10003
(212) 998-721

Ragan Report Workshops
407 South Dearborn Street
Chicago, IL 60605
(312) 922-8245

Stanford Communications Workshops
Publications Department
Stanford Alumni Association
Bauman Hose
Stanford, CA 94305
(415) 725-1083

U.S. Department of Agriculture Graduate School
Correspondence Study Program
South Agriculture Building
14th and Independence SW
Washington, DC 20250
(202) 447-7123

U.S. Department of Agriculture Graduate School
Office of Information and Public Affairs
600 Maryland Avenue SW
Room 129
Washington, DC 20024
(202) 447-4419

The University of Chicago
Publishing Program
5835 South Kimbark Avenue
Chicago, IL 60637
(312) 702-1722

Writers Center
Old Georgetown Road
Bethesda, MD 20814
(301) 654-8664

Grammar Hotlines

Following are some grammar hotlines listed alphabetically by state. The list is by no means complete, so if there is none listed for your area, check the *1993/94 Directory of Publications Resources* or with your local colleges to see if any of them run this kind of service.

Alabama

Grammar Hotline—(205) 348-5049, University of Alabama, Tuscaloosa, AL 35487

California

English Helpline—(916) 686-7444, Consumnes River College, 8401 Center Parkway, Sacramento, CA 95823

National Grammar Hotline—(805) 529-2321, Moorpark College, Moorpark, CA 93021

Canada

Grammar Hotline—(403) 450-4666, Grant MacEwan Community College, Edmonton, Alberta T5J 2P2

Grammar Hotline—(506) 453-4666 or 459-3631, University of New Brunswick, Fredericton, New Brunswick E3B 5A3

Colorado

USC Grammar Hotline—(303) 549-2787, University of Southern Colorado, Pueblo, CO 81001

Florida

Grammar Hotline—(305) 475-7697, University School of Nova University, Ft. Lauderdale, FL 33314

Writing Lab and Grammar Hotline—(904) 474-2129, University of West Florida, Pensacola, FL 32514

Illinois

Grammar Hotline—(217) 581-5929, Eastern Illinois University, Charleston, IL 61920

Grammar Hotline—(309) 438-2345, Illinois State University, Normal, IL 61761

Grammarline—(815) 224-2720, Illinois Valley Community College, Oglesby, IL 61348

Grammarphone—(312) 456-0300, Ext. 254, Triton College, River Grove, IL 60171

Indiana

Grammar Crisis Line—(317) 285-8387, Ball State University, The Writing Center, Muncie, IN 47306

Grammar Hotline—(317) 494-3723, Purdue University, West Lafayette, IN 47907

Louisiana

Grammar Hotline—(318) 231-5224, University of Southern Louisiana, Lafayette, LA 70504

Maryland

Grammarphone—(301) 689-4327, Frostburg State College, Frostburg, MD 21532

Massachusetts

Grammar Hotline—(617) 437-2512, Northeastern University, Boston, MA 02115

Grammar Hotline—(617) 593-7284, North Shore Community College, Lynn, MA 01901

Michigan

Grammar Hotline—(313) 762-0229, C.S. Mott Community College, Flint, MI 48503

Missouri

Grammar Hotline—(417) 624-0171, Missouri Southern State College, Joplin, MO 64801

New York

Rewrite—(718) 739-7483, York College of the City of New York, Jamaica, NY 11451

North Carolina

Grammar Hotline—(919) 488-7110, Methodist College, Fayetteville, NC 28301

Ohio

Dial-A-Grammar—(513) 745-5731, Raymond Walters College, Cincinnati, OH 45236

Grammar Hotline—(216) 972-7111, University of Akron, Akron, OH 44325

Grammar Hotline—(216) 987-2050, Cuyahoga Community College, Cleveland, OH 44122-6195

Oklahoma

Grammar Hotline—(405) 491-6328, Southern Nazarene University, Bethany, OK 73008

Pennsylvania

Grammar Hotline—(215) 932-8300, Ext. 460, Lincoln University, Lincoln University, PA 19352

Grammar Hotline—(412) 344-9759, Coalition for Adult Literacy, Pittsburgh, PA 15104

South Carolina

Grammar Hotline—(803) 792-3194, The Citadel Writing Center, Charleston, SC 29409

Grammar Hotline—(803) 596-9613, Converse College, Spartanburg, SC 29301

Texas

Grammarphone—(806) 374-4726, Amarillo College, Amarillo, TX 79178-0001

University of Houston Downtown Grammar Hotline—(713) 221-8670, University of Houston Downtown, Houston TX 77002

Virginia

Grammar Hotline—(804) 427-7170, Tidewater Community College Writing Center, Virginia Beach, VA 23456

Wisconsin

Grammar Hotline—(414) 498-5427, Northeast Wisconsin Technical Institute, Green Bay, WI 54307-9042

Grammar Hotline—(608) 342-1615, University of Wisconsin-Platteville, Platteville, WI 53818

Miscellaneous Services

This appendix contains the names and addresses of services such as sources of legal advice or help, business advice, job lines, even a specialty book store.

Association of the Bar of the City of New York, 42 West 44th Street, New York, NY 10036, Legal Referral Service, English, (212) 626-7373

California Lawyers for the Arts, San Francisco Office, Fort Mason Center, Building C, Room 255, San Francisco, CA 94123, (415) 775-7200

Columbus Society for the Communicating Arts, Columbus, OH, Hotline, (614) 766-3619

Community Free Job List (Deals with all types of jobs, not just editorial. You give them your phone number and when someone calls in looking for your type of service, they are given your number along with those of others with the same skills.) Columbus, OH, (614) 870-6460 (Tues.–Fri., 10:15 A.M.–3:00 P.M.)

Job Phone, Editorial Freelancers Association, 71 West 23rd Street, Suite 1504, New York, NY 10010, (212) 929-5400

Jobvine, Chicago Women in Publishing, 43 East Ohio Street, Suite 1022, Chicago, IL 60611, (312) 637-9038

Lawyers for the Creative Arts, 213 West Institute Place, Suite 411, Chicago, IL 60610-3125, (312) 944-ARTS

Recycled Software, (800) 851-2425

Small Business Administration, New York District Office, 26 Federal Plaza, New York, NY 10007, General Information, (212) 264-4354; Business Development, (212) 264-9487

Small Press Center, 20 West 44th Street, New York, NY 10036, (212) 764-7021

Tools of the Trade: Books for Communicators (a bookstore that specializes in books that deal with all areas of the publishing industry, including style manuals: write for a catalog), 3148-B Duke Street, Alexandria, VA 22314-4523, (703) 823-1919

U.S. Trademark Association, 1133 Avenue of the Americas, New York, NY 10036, (212) 768-9887

Volunteer Lawyers for the Arts, 1 East 53rd Street, New York, NY 10022, (212) 319-2787

Volunteer Lawyers for the Arts of Massachusetts, Inc., Office of Arts and Humanities, Boston City Hall, Room 716, Boston, MA 02201, (617) 523-1764

Women's Bureau, U.S. Department of Labor, Box BL, Washington, DC 20210

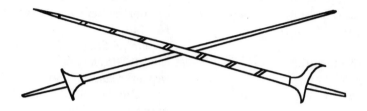

INDEX